The Librarian and Reference Queries

A SYSTEMATIC APPROACH

LIBRARY AND INFORMATION SCIENCE

CONSULTING EDITOR: *Harold Borko*
GRADUATE SCHOOL OF LIBRARY SCIENCE
UNIVERSITY OF CALIFORNIA, LOS ANGELES

Thomas H. Mott, Jr., Susan Artandi, and Leny Struminger
Introduction to PL/I Programming for Library and Information Scienc

Karen Sparck Jones and Martin Kay
Linguistics and Information Science

Manfred Kochen (Ed.)
Information for Action: From Knowledge to Wisdom

Harold Borko and Charles L. Bernier
Abstracting Concepts and Methods

G. Edward Evans
Management Techniques for Librarians

James Cabeceiras
The Multimedia Library: Materials Selection and Use

F. W. Lancaster
Toward Paperless Information Systems

H. S. Heaps
Information Retrieval: Computational and Theoretical Aspects

Harold Borko and Charles L. Bernier
Indexing Concepts and Methods

Gerald Jahoda and Judith Schiek Braunagel
The Librarian and Reference Queries: A Systematic Approach

in preparation
Charles H. Busha and Stephen P. Harter
Research Methods in Librarianship: Techniques and Interpretatio

The Librarian and Reference Queries

A SYSTEMATIC APPROACH

Gerald Jahoda

School of Library Science
The Florida State University
Tallahassee, Florida

Judith Schiek Braunagel

School of Information and Library Studies
State University of New York at Buffalo
Buffalo, New York

1980

Academic Press
A Subsidiary of Harcourt Brace Jovanovich, Publishers
New York London Toronto Sydney San Francisco

ACADEMIC PRESS, INC.
111 Fifth Avenue, New York, New York 10003

United Kingdom Edition published by
ACADEMIC PRESS, INC. (LONDON) LTD.
24/28 Oval Road, London NW1 7DX

Library of Congress Cataloging in Publication Data

Jahoda, Gerald
The librarian and reference queries.

(Library and information science)
Includes index.
1. Reference services (Libraries) I. Braunagel, Judith Schiek, joint author. II. Title. III. Series.
Z711.J34 025.5'2 79-6939
ISBN 0-12-379760-8

PRINTED IN THE UNITED STATES OF AMERICA

80 81 82 83 9 8 7 6 5 4 3 2 1

To Gloria Jahoda and David Braunagel

Contents

Preface

It is our belief that the teaching of reference work needs to revolve around practice in answering reference queries. After all, reference work is not a spectator sport. However, before students are given reference queries to answer, they need to be provided with a framework for doing so. The decision-making model of the reference process here provided is intended to offer such a framework. The model is based on work sponsored by the United States Office of Education and reported in Gerald Jahoda, *The Process of Answering Reference Questions: A Test of a Descriptive Model* (Final Report, Project No. 475AH50028, Grant No. G007500619). Washington, D.C.: United States Department of Health, Education and Welfare; Office of Education; and Office of Libraries and Learning Resources, 1977.

In the present text, students are introduced to the decision-making steps in a model of the reference process and are given exercises and answers for practicing each step. When students are familiar with each of the decision-making steps that make up the process of answering reference queries, they should be ready to search for answers to reference queries using a systematic approach. Exercises in answering reference queries are also given at the end of the book, with answers included to provide feedback. Emphasis is on the kinds of information included in types of reference tools, for example, encyclopedias, so that students can expect certain types of information in such tools when these tools are encountered in beginning as well as in advanced reference courses. A chapter on on-line searching has been included in the belief that this type of service is both related to reference work and is likely to be performed by more and more librarians during the coming years.

We suggest that the text be used in introductory reference courses. The content can be covered in one academic term with time for discussion of the role of reference work in libraries, networking and other forms of library cooperation, referral services, and discussion of specific reference titles. The text might also be used for in-service training of support personnel in libraries, or could be used for self-paced instruction of library personnel.

We are grateful to the Chemical Abstracts Service, the American Chemical Society, the Newspaper Enterprise Association, Inc., and to the Institute for Scientific Information for material reproduced herein. In addition to acknowledging the support of the United States Office of Education for the development of the model, we would like to thank our wife and husband, respectively, without whose encouragement, typing, and other assistance the text could not have been completed.

1

Introduction

The queries asked at a reference desk are unpredictable and vary from simple directional requests to elaborate research questions. Complex queries can involve considerable search time and the use of many reference sources. And a simple query can be difficult for the librarian considering it for the first time. Nevertheless, reference librarians are expected to answer unfamiliar or complex reference queries with the same skill they exercise for familiar or simple queries. Performing reference work requires more than learning a limited number of basic reference titles.

No librarian can remember all the reference resources both book and nonbook—such as films and recorded materials—that could satisfy a specific query, nor keep up with the constant flow of new materials. But with the aid of a logical approach for satisfying information requests the librarian can apply certain basic principles to locating an answer, regardless of the nature of the query asked or the library in which it is answered. This approach, based on an analysis of *the reference process*, involves interaction between the librarian, the library patron, and the library's resources in order to satisfy the patron's information need. With an understanding of the reference process, a librarian is not restricted to a limited number of reference materials but can apply general principles when answering unique or difficult requests.

In this text, the reference process has been broken down into a series of decision-making steps, ranging from receipt of an information request to communication of an answer. Each step is discussed in a separate chapter, followed by exercises to allow practice in the concepts presented. (A model of the reference process depicted as a series of decision-making steps is shown in Figure 1-1. This model, initially developed from a synthesis of several models of the reference process reported in the literature, has been further

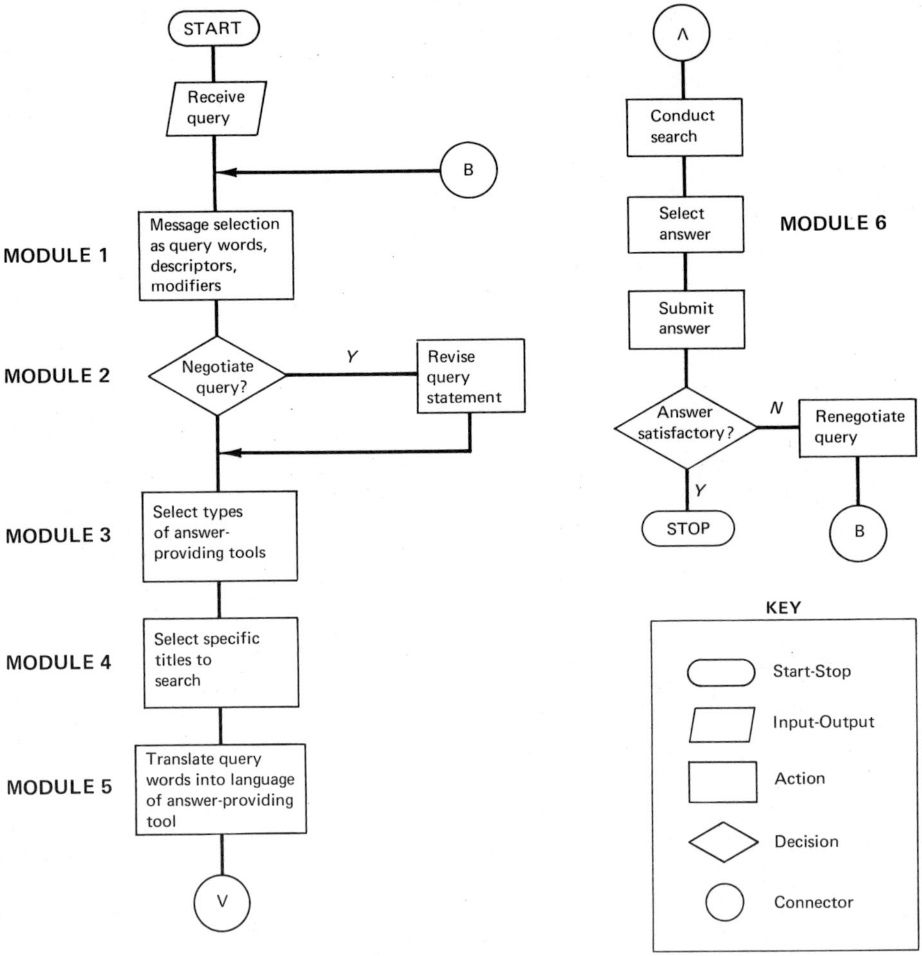

FIGURE 1-1

revised here based on testing and comments by practicing reference librarians.)

A MODEL OF THE REFERENCE PROCESS

The first decision-making step in the model, message selection, is identification of the essential information in the request of a library user. At this initial stage, the librarian analyzes the query to determine the subject of the request and to identify the type of information needed. The query may call for a fact, for example, the population of New York City in 1875, or one or more publications on a subject, for example, biographies of Martin Luther King, Jr. Once this step has been completed, the librarian must determine whether any clarification or amplification of the query is required. This process, called negotiation, requires discussion with the user about the request in order to gain a more complete understanding of the actual information need. If the librarian begins the search with an inaccurate understanding of what is really wanted, the information generated will be useless to the requestor. This wastes time for both, and may discourage the requestor from using reference services again.

Once the actual information need has been clarified through negotiation, the librarian can mentally identify categories of reference tools likely to contain the type of information needed. It is in this step that the reference librarian determines whether to search for the answer in a dictionary, an encyclopedia, or other type of reference tool. This step is followed by the selection of a specific title in which to begin searching for an answer to the query. If the librarian cannot remember a specific title in this category of reference tools, a specific German language dictionary for example, systematic techniques for identifying a specific title can be employed.

The fourth decision-making step involves location of an answer within the pages of the specific title selected. This is accomplished by selecting search headings which will provide access to information in that particular reference title. Selection of an answer, the final step, is crucial because the information identified in this step must be accurate and complete if it is to be useful to the requestor.

The process is completed when the information selected is communicated to the patron—but *only* if that information proves to be satisfactory to the patron. If not, the query is renegotiated, and the individual steps in the decision-making process are repeated.

Providing a complete and correct answer to an information request is dependent on the decisions made in each of the steps of the reference process. Errors at any of the decision-making points would result in an incorrect or inadequate answer. If the librarian misunderstands, the message of the query, he or she will end up searching for the wrong information. For example, a librarian might assume that the query, "Who wrote *Gone with the Wind*?" is a request for the name of the author of the book, *Gone with the Wind*, when what is really wanted in this case might be the author of the screenplay for the film of the same name. Such an error in message selection, the very first decision-making step, would result in an incorrect answer to the patron's real query. Similar errors could occur in any of the succeeding decision-making steps.

THE REFERENCE PROCESS

William Katz (1974) has defined the reference process as "the process of answering questions (p. xi)."[1] It might be defined even more generally as the process of satisfying specific, recurrent information needs. This is because some reference work, such as compiling bibliographies, may be performed in response to a generalized need on the part of many library users, rather than in response to a one-time-only question from a single user.

Although each librarian develops individual techniques and approaches to answer reference questions, it is important to attempt to isolate common characteristics of this process. While reference services may differ from library to library, the process of satisfying specific information needs probably remains essentially the same. In other words, the librarian answering the question of a fourth grader in a school library and the librarian locating information for a scientist in a special library each conduct their information search in similar ways. Both begin by extracting the essential information from the user's request, and both discuss, or negotiate, the query if clarification is necessary. Both librarians would then proceed in their searches following the same basic steps: identifying tools to search, locating the page or pages within the tool in which the answer is located, selecting the correct answer, and, finally, communicating the answer to the user and soliciting feedback.

This model of the reference process, the one used in this text, is only one of many speculative models of the process.[2] Many theories have been devel-

[1] Katz, William A. *Introduction to Reference Work*. Vol. 2, *Reference Services and Reference Processes*. New York: McGraw-Hill, 1974.

[2] Other models of the reference process include the following: Bunge, Charles A. *Reference Service in the Information Network*. A Paper for the Interlibrary Communications and Information Networks Conference, 1970. P. 8; Jahoda, Gerald and Olson, Paul E. "Analyzing the Reference Process." *RQ* **12** (1972): 148–156; Rees, Allan, and Saracevic, Tefko. "Conceptual Analysis of Questions in Information Retrieval Systems." *Annual Meeting of the American*

oped in an attempt to represent the process of answering reference queries in a concise and general way, illustrating the sequence of actions and decision points in the process. This model, like many others, has both strengths and weaknesses, and should be viewed as only one attempt to illustrate steps in the process. It has been selected for use in this text because it has been tested (and revised) based on comments from professional librarians, and because it provides a useful framework for studying components of the reference process.

It is important for several reasons that we understand how librarians go about satisfying reference requests. Reference librarians can apply this knowledge in analyzing their own work and in identifying aspects of their performance which could be strengthened or improved. Teachers of reference can utilize this knowledge to teach the process on a general level, in addition to familiarizing students with specific reference titles. Administrative personnel in reference departments would find this knowledge helpful when evaluating the performance of their reference staff. An understanding of the reference process also aids in determining which, if any, aspects of reference work can be delegated to support staff, or perhaps even to computers.

ARRANGEMENT OF THE TEXT

As previously stated, the chapters in this text are based on steps in the model of the reference process presented in Figure 1-1. In Chapter 2,"Message Selection," techniques are discussed for isolating the essential message of each query, and descriptors are presented to represent elements in the query message. In Chapters 3 and 4, categories of answer-providing reference tools are discussed, and a series of matrices are provided to aid in selection of a category of tool in which to search. Chapter 5 concentrates on the selection of specific titles to search, and discusses the use of the card catalog, guides to the literature, and bibliographies for identifying appropriate titles.

Chapters 6 and 7 deal with locating a correct answer in the specific title selected. Chapter 6 concentrates on selection of search headings for locating the page or pages which contain the answer, and Chapter 7 discusses techniques for providing an answer which is both correct and complete. Although negotiation appears following the message selection step in the model of the reference process, negotiation is discussed out of sequence, after the other steps of the process have been fully discussed. Clues for recognizing queries

---

Documentation Institute 1963, Part II, pp. 175–177; Shera, Jesse. "Automation and the Reference Librarian." *RQ* **3** (1964): 3–7; Stych, F. S. "The Flow Chart Method." *RQ* **5** (1966): 14–17.

that require negotiation are discussed in Chapter 8, and techniques for successful negotiation are presented in Chapter 9. Chapter 10 focuses on on-line searching of bibliographic data bases and discusses the characteristics of on-line searching along with an introduction to search logic. Chapter 11, a summary chapter, is followed by a section on actual reference queries asked in libraries and resources for locating answers to them.

ADDITIONAL READING

Holler, Frederick. "Toward a Reference Theory." *RQ* **14** (1975): 301–309.

Neill, S. G. "Problem Solving and the Reference Process." *RQ* **14** (1975): 310–315.

Rugh, Archie G. "Toward a Science of Reference Work: Basic Concepts." *RQ* **14** (1975): 293–300.

2

Message Selection

Imagine yourself on duty behind the reference desk. A library patron approaches you and asks, "Where is the *World Almanac*?" This is a simple query, to be sure, which will not tax your professional skills. Only in the unlikely case that your library does not have this basic reference source, or should the patron not be requesting what is really needed, will this type of request require more than a routine response (necessitating negotiation on your part). In this case, however, we will assume negotiation is not necessary and take the patron's words at face value in order to make some generalizations about this request.

First, throughout this text the library user's request for information will be called a query statement, or, more simply, a query. Specialized terms are necessary because in the reference dialogue *both* the patron and the librarian ask questions. The user asks questions related to his or her information need, and the librarian also asks questions during negotiation to determine exactly what the user wants. Therefore, in discussing the reference process it is necessary to differentiate between the user's questions and those of the librarian. It is for this reason that the user's initial question statement is called a query, while the librarian's query clarifications are termed questions.

THE QUERY MESSAGE

If we examine our sample query, "Where is the *World Almanac*?" we find that it contains two components. One component gives the subject of the information need (*World Almanac* in our example). The second component reveals the type of information needed about the subject (*Where is*—i.e., the location). Examination of hundreds of reference queries indicates that each query consists of at least those two components: the subject or "given" of the query and identification of the information needed about the subject (the "wanted"). Thus, each information request contains both a given and a wanted.

The following query is an example:

> *I am trying to locate the new address of one of my former college professors from Florida State University. Unfortunately, I have no idea where he is teaching now, but I think he's at some university in California. His name is Arthur Perkins, and he teaches botany.*

At first glance, this query may seem too complicated to be reduced to only two basic components, but it is possible to identify a single given and a single wanted.

"Arthur Perkins" is the subject, or given, of this query. The requestor has also provided us with some supplemental information about this person in addition to his name. He is a professor of botany who formerly taught at Florida State University, and who may now teach at a university in California. This supplementary information about Arthur Perkins will undoubtedly be helpful in the answer search, but none of these additional clues is very useful without the given, Arthur Perkins. It is true that a librarian could attempt to identify a professor of botany who formerly taught at Florida State University and who might presently work in some university in California, but it would be a lengthy and complicated search. It is this professor's name, Arthur Perkins, that is the true subject of the query, and thus we single it out as the given component.

Identifying the wanted component of this query is a simpler task. The requestor is asking for Arthur Perkins' current address. Thus, this seemingly lengthy query can be simplified into two components: the requestor wants the *address* of *Arthur Perkins*. It is possible to dissect any query, no matter how complicated, in this manner.

A query may appear more difficult to break down into a single given and wanted because the query is actually comprised of two separate queries. For example:

> *What is the life span of the sparrow, and what do their nests look like?*

In this two-query request, the first given is "sparrow" and the wanted is "life span." The second given is also sparrow, and the wanted is a description or illustration of a sparrow's nest.

UTILIZING THE MESSAGE IN SUBSEQUENT DECISION-MAKING STEPS

The given and the wanted represent the message, or the essential information, contained in a query. Other supplementary information may be included, as illustrated in the example, but would be useless without the essential message of the query. Learning to isolate the message in each query is an aid to answering queries correctly in several ways. First, it helps to identify queries that require negotiation before you can proceed with an answer search. Second, it is an aid in selecting types of reference tools to search, and will provide points of entry for searching the titles selected.

If, in analyzing a query, you decide that either the given or the wanted is unclear or absent, it is a clue that negotiation will be necessary before beginning the search. Because an error in the message selection step will result in compounded errors throughout the succeeding steps of the process, it is important to clarify the given and wanted before proceeding. In addition, certain types of givens and wanteds provide clues that indicate the real query may not have been asked. This aspect of the query message will be discussed more fully in the chapter on negotiation.

The given and wanted can assist in identifying types of reference tools likely to contain answers to a query, as categories of reference tools can also be generally grouped in terms of givens and wanteds. (This will be discussed in greater detail later in this chapter.) Once a specific title has been selected, the given may also function as a search heading, or access point, for searching the title.

EXERCISE 1 Selection of the Given and Wanted of a Query

(For each of the queries below, identify the given and wanted component.)

Query	*Given*	*Wanted*
SAMPLE QUERY: *Do you have any lists of publications about Niagara Falls?*	Niagara Falls	List of publications
1. "What does entropy mean?"		
2. "What is Christian Dior's address?"		
3. "What is the circulation of *Newsweek?*"		
4. "Where can I find a picture of Joseph Sabin?"		
5. "When was the American Library Association founded?"		
6. "Who invented the steam engine?"		
7. "How many calories are there in an avocado?"		
8. "Can you recommend a good book on needlecraft?"		

Answers are on pp. 15–16.

Message selection, then, is not an end in itself, but a single step in the total process of answering queries. Selection of the given and wanted is an important mental exercise which will become internalized and automatic as one accumulates experience in answering reference queries.

MESSAGE DESCRIPTORS

As you can imagine, there are as many potential givens and wanteds as there are query statements. Requests for the addresses of Arthur Perkins, Alexis Smith, and Gloria O'Connor, for example, result in three different givens. This is because we have selected the given in terms of the words used in the query. In actuality, these are three queries with the *same type* of given—the name of a person. Similarly, in the queries "Who invented the

TABLE 2-1
Checklist of Given and Wanted Descriptors

Given	Wanted
Abbreviation	Date
Organization (specifically named)	Illustration
Person (specifically named)	Numeric information
Place (specifically named)	Properties (scientifically measured)
Term or subject (other than specific types already listed)	Statistics (involves counting)
Specific publication	Organization
	Person
	Address or general location
	Publication
	Bibliography
	Document location
	Verification or completion of bibliographic data
	Textual information
	Definition–Symbol
	Recommendation
	General or background information

light bulb?" and "What is the full name of the president of the American Library Association?" the same type of wanted can be identified—again, the name of a person. Most givens and wanteds can be more generally classified in terms of a limited number of indexing terms called descriptors. A list of these descriptors is presented in Table 2-1.

Using this table, we can translate the requests for the location of the *World Almanac* and for the address of Arthur Perkins into more general descriptors. The given descriptor for *World Almanac* is "specific publication"; the wanted descriptor that applies is "address or general location." In the request for the address of Arthur Perkins, the given name, Arthur Perkins, can be replaced by the given descriptor, "person," and we find that the wanted descriptor is, in this example too, "address or general location."

By categorizing the givens and wanteds from query statements into general descriptors, we can *group* similar queries together, and can often approach their answer searches in similar ways. Many reference librarians mentally select categories of reference tools, such as dictionaries or encyclopedias, that would likely contain an answer. Selection of suitable categories of answer providing tools can be performed by becoming familiar with the types of given and wanted information found in such types of tools.

A suitable answer to a query may thus be seen as a mental match between the message of the query and the probable types of information provided by specific types of reference sources. This process will be thoroughly discussed in Chapter 3.

GIVENS AND WANTEDS

Brief definitions of the given and wanted descriptors and examples of their use follow.

Givens

1. *Abbreviation*: Use when an abbreviation or symbol is given.
   Examples: "What does *ibid.* mean in a footnote?"
   "What does ♂ mean?"
2. *Organization* (specifically named): Use when the name of a company, government agency, library, school, or other organization is given.
   Example: "Where are the National Institutes of Health?"
3. *Person* (specifically named): Use when the name of an individual is given.
   Example: "When was Nelson Rockefeller born?"
4. *Place* (specifically named): Use when a specific place name is given and information about that place is wanted.
   Example: "Where is Loch Ness?"
5. *Term or subject*: Use when information about a word or subject is wanted and the word or subject cannot be characterized by another descriptor on the checklist.
   Example: "I want background information on modern poetry."
6. *Specific publication*: Use when the title of a specific book, journal, report, dissertation, or other publication is fully or partially cited.
   Example: "Do you have *American Heritage*?"

Wanteds

7. *Date*: Use when either a specific date or a time period is wanted.
   Examples: "When was the first cyclotron built?"
   "When was the Industrial Revolution?"

8. *Illustration*: Use when a picture, map, or any other type of illustration is wanted.
   Examples: "I would like to look at a photograph of Harry Truman.
   "Do you have a map of St. Petersburg, Florida?"

9. *Numeric information*: (Two descriptors are provided):

   9a. *Measurements*
   Example: "What is the air mileage between New York and Washington, D.C.?"

   9b. *Counting various units*
   Example: "How many full-time students were enrolled at SUNY/Buffalo in September, 1976?"

10. *Organization*: Use when the name of a company, government agency, library, academic institution, or other organization is wanted.
    Example: "Who manufactures camping lanterns?"

11. *Person*: Use when the name of an individual is wanted.
    Example: "Who invented Xerography?"

12. *Address or general location*: Use when either address or location is wanted.
    Examples: "What is the address of Leonard Bernstein?"
    "Where is Mount Everest?"

13. *Publication*: Three descriptors dealing with wanted publications are used.

    13a. *Bibliography*: Use when only a list of bibliographic citations is wanted.
    Example: "I need a list of references on growing orchids."

    13b. *Document location*: Use for location of specifically identified titles in local or other libraries.
    Example: "Where is the July, 1956 issue of *Atlantic Monthly*?"

    13c. *Verification or completion of bibliographic data:*
    Use for a verification of a complete or partially given citation.
    Example: "Can you locate the full citation for the following:
    C. Mooers, *Aslib Proc.* 1956."

14. *Textual information*: Three descriptors specify the amount of textual information wanted.

    14a. *Definition–symbol*: Use when definition of terms or identification of symbols is wanted.
    Example: "What does the abbreviation 'e.g.' mean?"

14b. *Recommendation*: Use when appraisal or review of a publication, film, product, etc. is wanted.
Example: "What is a good book for a teenage girl who wants to read about horses?"

14c. *General or background information*: Use when the requested answers are documents or summaries of documents, or when the requestor wants introductory or background information on a topic.
Example: "I want journal articles and books on the history of Liberia."

SUMMARY

In this chapter we have characterized the message of each query as the subject of the query, the *given*, and the information needed about the subject, the *wanted*. Next, the specific message words used by the requestor in a query have been translated into generic tags called given and wanted *descriptors*. Each query can be divided into these two components, although not all queries may be indexed with the list of descriptors on the checklist. In the following chapter, we shall use the descriptors identified for a specific query as an aid in selecting types of answer-providing tools in which to search for an answer.

QUESTIONS FOR DISCUSSION

Differentiate between message words used in a query statement and descriptors.

Differentiate between givens and wanteds.

Can you think of specific queries that could not be indexed with the list of descriptors?

Could the message selection step be performed by clerks or computers? What about selection of descriptors?

The following exercise is intended to familiarize you with the list of given and wanted descriptors.

EXERCISE 2 Selection of Given and Wanted Descriptors

(For each query, select a given and wanted descriptor from the descriptor lists.)

Query	*Given*	*Wanted*
SAMPLE QUERY: *What is the weight of an adult zebra?*	Term–Subject	Numeric information—Measurement
1. "Which professional society uses the following abbreviation: ASIS?"		
2. "What is the size of Lake Michigan?"		
3. "When was the painter Pierre Auguste Renoir born?"		
4. "Describe what Lions Clubs do."		
5. "What is the address of the American Chemical Society?"		
6. "I need citations for a paper on women's rights."		
7. "What does LPG mean?"		
8. "Where can I get copies of *Psychology Today*?"		

Answers are on p. 16.

ANSWERS

Exercise 1

Query	*Given*	*Wanted*
1.	entropy	definition
2.	Christian Dior	address
3.	*Newsweek*	circulation

Query	*Given*	*Wanted*
4.	Joseph Sabin	picture
5.	American Library Association	when founded
6.	steam engine	inventor (who invented)
7.	avocado	number of calories
8.	needlecraft	recommended book

Exercise 2

Query	*Given*	*Wanted*
1.	Abbreviation	Organization
2.	Place	Numeric information—measurement
3.	Person	Date
4.	Organization	Background information
5.	Organization	Address–Location
6.	Term–Subject	Bibliography
7.	Abbreviation	Definition–Symbol
8.	Specific publication	Document location

3

Selection of Categories of Answer-Providing Tools

In the last chapter, we discussed the process of selecting the message from a query, and translating it into given and wanted descriptors. If the query does not require negotiation, the next step in the reference process is usually selection of categories of reference tools likely to contain an answer. Although the experienced librarian in a single mental operation probably combines this step with the next, identification of specific titles, we will discuss each step separately as an aid in learning the process.

Some types of queries are asked repeatedly at a reference desk. Requests for the mailing address of a local congressman, for the names of presidents of corporations, or for information on filing income tax returns may be asked by many people in a single day. When asked a familiar query, the librarian is able to go directly to a specific title with confidence that it contains a satisfactory answer. In trying to answer queries they have never answered before, however, some librarians think first in terms of types of reference tools likely to contain answers. While there are thousands of individual reference titles, most of these titles can be categorized into a limited number of general groups. Individual titles within each category share certain basic characteristics and contain similar types of information. A list of categories of reference tools is given in Table 3-1.

TABLE 3-1
Categories of Answer-Providing Tools

Biographical sources
Card catalogs; union lists
Dictionaries
Encyclopedias
Geographical sources
Guides to the literature
Handbooks; manuals
Indexes; bibliographies; abstracts
Monographs; texts
Nonbiographical directories
Primary publications
Yearbooks; almanacs

After isolating categories of reference sources likely to contain satisfactory answers, the librarian can proceed to select a specific title from that category of reference sources. To perform this step, the experienced reference librarian probably associates the type of information requested in the query with types, or categories, of reference sources available, making a mental match between the patron's information need and the expected content of certain categories of tools. Like queries, which can be characterized by givens and wanteds, each group of reference tools can be categorized by combinations of givens and wanteds.

DESCRIPTOR AND TOOL TABLES

Tables 3-2 through 3-7 provide a mental aid for matching the message of the query with the content of categories of reference tools. In these Tables a given descriptor is combined with individual wanted descriptors, and the types of tools likely to satisfy each combination are itemized. These tables were prepared by indexing the general content of each tool category with given and wanted descriptors. There is no limitation on the number of descriptors that can be used to index the content of each tool category, which differs from indexing the message in a query in which there is only one given descriptor and one wanted descriptor.

The following example illustrates the use of the tables.

QUERY: *Is there a garden club in Atlanta?*

QUERY MESSAGE: given—*Atlanta*
wanted—*Garden club*

DESCRIPTORS: given—*Term–Subject*
wanted—*Organization*

Examine Table 3-6, p. 23, for the given descriptor, "Term–Subject." When combined with the wanted descriptor, "Organization," the suggested category of answer-providing tool is "Nonbiographical directories." Nonbiographical directories provide information about organizations, clubs, business firms and associations, and may focus on a local area or a larger geographic area, such as a state or nation.

The following is another example of use of the tables.

QUERY: *Where can I find some historical information about Florida State University?*

QUERY MESSAGE: given—*Florida State University*
wanted—*Historical information*

DESCRIPTORS: given—*Organization*
wanted—*Background information*

In Table 3-3, "Organization" as a given descriptor lists the following categories of tools for a "background information" request:

Encyclopedia
Handbook; manual
Monograph; text
Nonbiographical directory
Primary publication

(In our first query, notice that a single category of answer-providing tools is available, while several are listed for the second query.)

In trying to satisfy a patron's request (such as historical information about Florida State University) by using Table 3-3 as a guide, a method is needed to choose a sequence for searching each tool category. There is undoubtedly an optimum search sequence, but the present level of knowledge

TABLE 3-2
Given: Abbreviation–Symbol
Example: A.L.A.,♀

Wanted	Sample query	Type of tool
Organization	"What does A.L.A. stand for?"	Dictionary
Definition	"What does this symbol mean: ♀?"	Dictionary; handbook; manual

TABLE 3-3
Given: Organization
Example: Library of Congress

Wanted	Sample query	Type of tool
Date	"When was the Library of Congress established?"	Encyclopedia Nonbiographical directory Monograph; text
Illustration	"I'd like to see a photograph of the Library of Congress reading room."	Encyclopedia Monograph; text Primary publication
Numeric information—measurement	"How many square feet are there in the Library of Congress reading room?"	Encyclopedia Monograph; text Primary publication
Numeric information—counting	"How many titles does the Library of Congress catalog each year?"	Encyclopedia Nonbiographical directory Primary publication
Organization	"To which branch of government does the Library of Congress report?"	Nonbiographical directory
Person	"Who is the current Librarian of Congress?"	Encyclopedia Monograph; text Nonbiographical directory
Address–Location	"What is the mailing address of the Library of Congress?"	Encyclopedia Guide to the literature Handbook; manual Nonbiographical directory
Bibliography	"Do you have a list of Library of Congress publications?"	Card catalog; union list Index; bibliography; abstract
Document Location	"Do you have a copy of the most recent Library of Congress annual report?"	Card catalog; union list
Document verification	"Give complete citation for a book about the Library of Congress by Salamanca."	Card catalog; union list Index; bibliography; abstract
Background information	"Who is eligible to use the reading room of the Library of Congress?"	Encyclopedia Handbook; manual Monograph; text Nonbiographical directory Primary publication

TABLE 3-4
Given: Person
Example: Harry Truman

Wanted	Sample query	Type of tool
Date	"When was Harry Truman born"	Biographical source Dictionary Encyclopedia
Illustration	"I'd like to see a photograph of Harry Truman."	Biographical source Encyclopedia Monograph; text Yearbook; almanac
Numeric information—measurement	"How tall was Harry Trumann?"	Biographical source Encyclopedia Monograph; text Yearbook; almanac
Numeric information—counting	"How old was Harry Truman when he became President?"	Biographical source Encyclopedia Monograph; text Yearbook; almanac
Organization	"What church did Harry Truman attend?"	Biographical source Encyclopedia
Person	"What are the names of Harry Truman's parents?"	Biographical source Encyclopedia Monograph; text
Address–Location	"Where was Harry Truman born?"	Biographical source Encyclopedia Monograph; text
Bibliography	"I have to do a report on Harry Truman, and need some books on him."	Biographical source Card catalog; union list Index; bibliography; abstract
Document verification	"What was the title of Harry Truman's autobiography?"	Card catalog; union list Index; bibliography; abstract
Background information	"I'd like some information on Harry Truman's Presidency."	Biographical source Encyclopedia Monograph; text Primary publication Yearbook; almanac

TABLE 3-5
Given: Address–Location
Example: Washington, D.C.

Wanted	Sample query	Type of tool
Date	"When was the city of Washington established?"	Encyclopedia Geographical source Monograph; text
Illustration	"I'd like to see a map of downtown Washington."	Encyclopedia Geographical source Monograph; text
Numeric information—measurement	"How far is Washington from Baltimore?	Encyclopedia Geographical source
Numeric information—counting	"What is the population of Washington, D.C.?"	Encyclopedia Geographical source Primary publication
Organization	"What art museums are located in Washington?"	Nonbiographical directory
Person	"Who is the current mayor of Washington?"	Encyclopedia Geographical source
Address–Location	"What states border Washington, D.C.?"	Encyclopedia Geographical source
Bibliography	"I'd like a list of novels set in Washington, D.C."	Card catalog; union list Index; bibliography; abstract

in reference has not yet provided for any generalizations about the best sequence for searching potentially useful reference tools. This is an area for needed research in reference work.

All things being equal, the optimum search sequence should provide the most complete answer in the least time. Thus, if there is a choice between using a familiar encyclopedia with a known location and trying another, unfamiliar type of tool that would have to be located in the card catalog, a text for example, then the encyclopedia would probably be the best first tool to search. If the patron wants to borrow the document, however, the text might be the better choice even though it would take more time to locate it.

TABLE 3-6
Given: Term–Subject
Example: Baseball

Wanted	Sample query	Type of tool
Date	"When was the game of baseball invented?"	Dictionary Encyclopedia Handbook; manual Monograph; text
Illustration	"Can you locate an early photograph of a professional baseball game?"	Dictionary Encyclopedia Handbook; manual Monograph; text
Numeric information—measurement	"What are the dimensions of a regulation baseball diamond?"	Dictionary Encyclopedia Handbook; manual
Numeric information—counting	"How many professional baseball games are played in the U.S. annually?"	Encyclopedia Handbook; manual Yearbook; almanac
Organization	"What organization coordinates Little League baseball in the U.S.?"	Nonbiographical directory
Person	"Who invented baseball?"	Encyclopedia Yearbook; almanac
Address–Location	"Where was baseball invented?"	Encyclopedia Monograph; text
Bibliography	"I need some information on baseball for a term paper I'm writing."	Card catalog; union list Guide to the literature Index; bibliography; abstract
Document verification	"Who wrote a book on baseball called *Ball Four*?"	Card catalog; union list Index; bibliography; abstract
Recommendation	"Could you suggest a good book on baseball for a 14-year-old boy?"	Index; bibliography; abstract
Background information	"How do the rules of baseball differ from those of cricket?"	Encyclopedia Handbook; manual Monograph; text

TABLE 3-7
Given: Specific Publication
Example: *Scientific American*

Wanted	Sample query	Type of tool
Date	"When did *Scientific American* begin publication?"	Card catalog; union list Index; bibliography; abstract
Numeric information—counting	"How many issues of *Scientific American* are published each year?"	Index; bibliography; abstract Primary publication
Organization	"What company publishes *Scientific American*?"	Card catalog; union list Index; bibliography; abstract
Person	"Who is the editor of *Scientific American*?"	Card catalog; union list Index; bibliography; abstract Primary publication
Address–Location	"Where can I write to *Scientific American*?"	Index; bibliography; abstract
Bibliography	"Has *Scientific American* published any articles on ecology in the last 3 years?"	Card catalog; union list Guide to the literature Index; bibliography; abstract
Document location	"What is the call number for *Scientific American*?"	Card catalog; union list
Document verification	"What volume number was the July 1974 issue of *Scientific American*?"	Card catalog; union list Index; bibliography; abstract Primary publication
Background information	"What is the editorial policy of *Scientific American*?"	Card catalog; union list Index; bibliography; abstract Primary publication

SUMMARY

Although there are thousands of individual reference titles, titles with similar characteristics can be grouped together in general categories. Within the same category, titles tend to contain similar types of information content which can be summarized using given and wanted descriptors. This allows us to match query descriptors with the reference-tool descriptors and select a category of tools to search. The query and reference-tool descriptor tables (Tables 3-2 through 3-7) have been developed to assist you in this matching process by referring you to one or more types of tools likely to include an answer for a query which has been indexed with a specific combination of given and wanted descriptors.

A word of caution is in order: The tables are "suggestive" rather than "prescriptive." They do not include every possible type of reference tool applicable to a specific query, and the suggested type or types of answer-providing tools may not yield an answer. The tables are intended to serve as a learning aid. After some practice in answering reference queries, you will probably internalize this matching process and automatically associate a type of query with one or more types of answer-providing tools, and customize it according to your needs.

QUESTIONS FOR DISCUSSION

What abilities or skills do you feel a reference librarian needs to be able to locate answers to queries of varied complexity and in diverse subject areas?

As a practicing reference librarian, what will you do to keep aware of the continuous flow of new reference titles?

EXERCISE Selection of Categories of Answer-Providing Tools

(For each query below, identify the wanted and given descriptors, and use the tables to identify a category or categories of tool to search.)

1. "What is the mailing address of the United Nations?"
2. "I need a list of Hemingway's novels, and the year when each was published."
3. "Where did the quote, 'Know thyself,' come from?"
4. "What is the address of Lafayette College in Pennsylvania?"

5. "When did Paul Robeson die?"
6. "Who was the real life prototype for the character of the writer in Somerset Maugham's *Cake and Ale*?"
7. "What is Lady Bird Johnson's real first name?"
8. "Could you give me the names of all daily newspapers published in Rome, Italy?"
9. "What is the maximum income a person can make and not have to file an income tax return?"
10. "I need information on how to celebrate a fiftieth wedding anniversary."

Answers to exercise are on p. 26.

ANSWERS TO EXERCISE

(Note: Numbers in parentheses refer to the definitions given in Chapter 2)

1. *Given*: Organization (2)
   Wanted: Address–General location (12)
   Categories of tools: Encyclopedias
   Guides to the literature
   Handbooks; manuals
   Nonbiographical directories

2. *Given*: Person (3)
   Wanted: Bibliography (13a)
   Categories of tools: Biographical sources
   Card catalog; union lists
   Indexes; bibliographies; abstracts

3. *Given*: Term or subject (5)
   Wanted: General or background information (14b)
   Categories of tools: Encyclopedias
   Handbooks; manuals
   Monographs; texts

4. *Given*: Organization (2)
   Wanted: Address–General location (12)
   Categories of tools: Encyclopedias
   Guides to the literature
   Handbooks; manuals
   Nonbiographical directories

5. *Given*: Person (3)
   Wanted: Date (7)
   Categories of tools: Biographical sources
   Dictionaries
   Encyclopedias

6. *Given*: Specific publication (6)
   Wanted: Person (11)
   Categories of tools: Card catalog; union lists
   Indexes; bibliographies; abstracts
   Primary publications

7. *Given*: Person (3)
   Wanted: General or background information (14b)
   Categories of tools: Biographical sources
   Encyclopedias
   Monographs; texts
   Primary publications
   Yearbooks; almanacs

8. *Given*: Place (4)
   Wanted: Bibliography (13a)
   Categories of tools: Card catalog; union lists
   Indexes; bibliographies; abstracts

9. *Given*: Term or subject (5)
   Wanted: Statistics (9b)
   Categories of tools: Encyclopedias
   Handbooks; manuals
   Yearbooks; almanacs

10. *Given*: Term or subject (5)
    Wanted: General or background information (14b)
    Categories of tools: Encyclopedias
    Handbooks; manuals
    Monographs; texts

4

Categories of Answer-Providing Tools

In the preceding chapter, we discussed the use of given and wanted descriptors in selection of categories of reference tools likely to contain an answer to a query. This process involves matching the query message with types of information frequently contained in specific categories of reference tools. We now turn to a detailed description of these categories. To begin with, each category has a list of given and wanted descriptors used to index a title. (These combinations of given and wanted descriptors are reflected in the tables in Chapter 3.)

BIOGRAPHICAL SOURCES

Biographical sources are reference tools that provide information about people. They are frequently called either biographical dictionaries or biographical directories because they are often arranged in a dictionary or directory format.

Biographical sources differ in terms of the amount of information given about each person listed. At a minimum, only the name and address of each individual would be provided. Other biographical sources may provide additional information about each person, including his or her date of birth, professional and avocational pursuits, memberships in organizations, and publications. Biographical sources are usually arranged alphabetically by last name, but may also contain classified indexes, such as an index by geographical location or by profession. In addition, biographical sources also vary in terms of time period covered, criteria for inclusion, and style of presentation.

DESCRIPTORS FOR BIOGRAPHICAL SOURCES

Given

Person (3)[1]

Wanted

Date (7)
Illustration (8)

TABLE 4-1
Sample Reference Source: Biographical

Title	*Current Biography*
Coverage	Includes biographical articles about leaders in all fields of human endeavor, living anywhere in the world.
Organization	Alphabetical by name of person.
Given descriptors	Person (3)
Wanted descriptors	Date (7) Organization (10) Person (11) Address; general location (12) Bibliography (13a) General or background information (14c)
SAMPLE QUERY	*How long has Walter Cronkite been anchorman for the CBS Evening News?*
	ACCESS POINT: Cronkite, Walter (Leland, Jr.)
	ANSWER: Cronkite has been anchorman for the *CBS Evening News* since 1962.[a]

[a] From *Current Biography Yearbook, 1975*. New York: H. W. Wilson 1975. P. 95.

[1] Numbers in parentheses refer to list of definitions of given and wanted descriptors presented in Chapter 2.

Organization (10)
Person (11)
Address–Location (12)
Bibliography (13a)
Background information (14c)

Table 4-1 gives a sample biographical reference source.

CARD CATALOG; UNION LISTS

A library card catalog lists the titles held in a specific library collection. It is the most common form of catalog used in libraries today. Entries for library holdings are placed on separate cards, which are usually arranged in alphabetical order. The union list records the holdings of a given group of libraries. It may be a general list or restricted to materials in a certain field, on a particular subject, or of a given type of publication such as a union list of serials.

Both the card catalog and the union list can function as location devices, or lead-in tools, by directing the user to sources of information on a subject, but not the information itself. The card catalog enables the user who knows the author, title, or subject area of the material to discern whether his or her library holds it and where it can be found. A union list locates those libraries which do hold copies.

DESCRIPTORS FOR CARD CATALOGS AND UNION LISTS

Given

Organization (2)
Person (3)
Place (4)
Term–Subject (5)
Specific publication (6)

Wanted

Date (7)
Organization (10)
Person (11)
Bibliography (13a)
Document location (13b)
Document verification (13c)

Table 4-2 gives a sample union list reference source.

TABLE 4-2
Sample Reference Source: Union List

Title	*New Serial Titles*
Coverage	Lists serials first published after December 31, 1949 which have been received by the Library of Congress or by cooperating libraries. Exclusions include newspapers, looseleaf publications, and municipal government serials. Serves as a supplement to the *Union List of Serials*. When available, the following information is given for serial entries: name of issuing body; place of publication; beginning and ending dates; and holdings of cooperative libraries.
Organization	Alphabetical by serial entry
Given descriptors	Specific publication (6)
Wanted descriptors	Date (7) Numeric information—counting (9b) Organization (10) Address–Location (12) Document location (13b) Document verification (13c) Background information (14c)
SAMPLE QUERY	*Do any libraries in Florida receive the* ***Arkansas River Review****?* ACCESS POINT: *Arkansas River Review* ANSWER: Yes. Both the University of Florida (FU) and Florida State University (FlaSU) have received it since the first volume was issued.[a]

[a] From *New Serial Titles: A Union List Serials Commencing Publication After December 31, 1949*. (3rd ed. 1971–1974 cumulation). Washington, D.C.: Library of Congress, 1975. Vol. 1; p. 129.

DICTIONARIES

A dictionary is a word or term book. The words included in a dictionary may be those of a language (or languages, as in a bilingual or polyglot dictionary), or the terms used in a specific discipline (a special subject dictionary such as a chemical dictionary). These words or terms are arranged in a definite order, usually alphabetical, and varied amounts of information are given about them.

We have all used an English language dictionary to look up the meaning of a word, its spelling, or pronunciation. For instance, if we look up "photosynthesis" in a general language dictionary we would find the proper spelling, its pronunciation, and a brief definition of the term. In addition to spelling, pronunciation, and meaning, a general language dictionary may also include information on a word's history, its use, abbreviations, synonyms, and

TABLE 4-3
Sample Reference Source: Dictionary

Title	*A Dictionary of Slang and Unconventional English*
Coverage	Includes terms and phrases of slang, colloquialisms, catch-phrases, nicknames, and vulgarisms. Sample entries include: "Legal eagle" (a lawyer) "No soap" (no hope) "On the fritz" (broken) For terms and phrases, definition, usage, and origins are given.
Organization	In the seventh edition, the basic dictionary and its supplement are in one volume. Alphabetical dictionary arrangement of terms and phrases, with cross-references.
Given descriptors	Term–Subject (5)
Wanted descriptors	Date (7) Address–Location (12) Definition–Symbol (14a) Background information (14c)
SAMPLE QUERY	*How did the phrase* ***Kilroy was here*** *originate?* (It is usually accompanied by a sketch of a man peering over a wall.) ACCESS POINT: Kilroy was here ANSWER: Many explanations have been offered for the origin of this phrase and drawing. During World War II it was frequently found written on walls in areas where British or American soldiers were located. One suggested explanation of its origin cites an inspector in a shipyard named James J. Kilroy who left it on equipment as his mark of inspection.[a]

[a] From Partridge, Eric; *A Dictionary of Slang and Unconventional English.* 7th ed. New York: Macmillan, 1970. Pp. 1236–1237.

antonyms. Some dictionaries will also include encyclopedic information, such as illustrations, charts, grammatical rules, biographical information on individuals, and geographical information on places.

The scope of the special subject dictionary is usually limited to giving pronunciation and definitions for the specialized terms in a discipline. Frequently the terms in a special subject dictionary cannot be adequately defined using a general language dictionary because of their currency, specificity, or unique use within a certain field.

DESCRIPTORS FOR DICTIONARIES

Given

Abbreviation–Symbol (1)
Person (3)

Place (4)
Term–Subject (5)

Wanted

Illustration (8)
Numeric information—measurement (9a)
Numeric information—counting (9b)
Organization (10)
Address–Location (12)
Definition–Symbol (14a)

Table 4-3 gives a sample dictionary reference source.

ENCYCLOPEDIAS

Encyclopedias tend to fall into two basic categories: general and special subject. The general encyclopedia includes articles on subjects in every field of knowledge; the special subject encyclopedia concentrates on a single area or discipline. Encyclopedic information tends to be written in a narrative style and can be quite detailed and lengthy, depending on the audience for which the encyclopedia has been written.

In a general adult encyclopedia, if we look up "photosynthesis" we would probably find a detailed discussion of the process. Beginning with a brief definition, the encyclopedia might go on to include a description of the importance of photosynthesis to life cycles on earth, influences on the rate of photosynthesis, components of the process, and research on the topic. In addition, the encyclopedia article might include diagrams, chemical equations, and a short bibliography.

The specialized encyclopedia is often written for a person knowledgeable in the field and will typically provide more highly detailed or sophisticated coverage of the subject than the general encyclopedia (which is aimed at nonspecialists). In other cases, a concept or term described in a specialized subject encyclopedia may be completely omitted from a general encyclopedia.

DESCRIPTORS FOR ENCYCLOPEDIAS

Given

Organization (2)
Person (3)
Place (4)
Term–Subject (5)

TABLE 4-4
Sample Reference Source: Encyclopedia

Title	*Encyclopedia of Library and Information Science*
Coverage	Includes information related to information science and librarianship. Sample subject headings include: Hospital libraries and collections Machine translation Decision making Name entries include those for people, publications, and places. Examples: *Horn Book Magazine* Hutchins, Margaret Iceland, Libraries in
Organization	Alphabetic dictionary arrangement of subjects and names.
Given descriptors	Organization (2) Person (3) Place (4) Term–Subject (5) Specific publication (6)
Wanted descriptors	Date (7) Illustration (8) Numeric information—measurement (9a) Numeric information—counting (9b) Organization (10) Person (11) Address–Location (12) Bibliography (13a) Definition–Symbol (14a) Background information (14c)
SAMPLE QUERY	*What is a fore-edge painting?* ACCESS POINT: Fore-edge painting ANSWER: A painting on the fore edge of a book that can be seen when the leaves are fanned and is invisible when the book is closed. Illustrations of fore-edge paintings are included in the article.[a]

[a] From Kent, Allen, Lancour Harold, and Daily, Jay E., (Eds.), *Encyclopedia of Library and Information Science*. (24 volumes up to 1978.) New York: Marcel Dekker, 1968. Volume 9, p. 1.

Wanted

Date (7)
Illustration (8)
Numeric information—measurement (9a)
Numeric information—counting (9b)
Organization (10)
Person (11)
Address–Location (12)
Bibliography (13a)
Definition–Symbol (14a)
Background information (14c)

Table 4-4 gives a sample encyclopedia reference source.

GEOGRAPHICAL SOURCES

Geographical sources are reference tools that provide information about places, and include atlases, maps, gazetteers, and guidebooks. Each of these categories provides a different type of information about places.

Gazetteers

A gazetteer is a geographic dictionary which, alphabetically, lists places and physical features giving concise information about them. If, for instance, you looked up "Rome" in a gazetteer, you would find it listed before "Rome City, Indiana" and after the "Rombo Islands." You would also find several listings for Rome: one for Rome, Italy, and others for cities named Rome in Georgia, Illinois, Iowa, Maine, Mississippi, New York, Ohio, and Pennsylvania.

The amount of information given for each place listed in a gazetteer varies. For "Rome, Italy" the information provided would be quite extensive, while for the various cities named Rome throughout the United States it would be more brief. The kinds of information a gazetteer may provide about a place include the spelling and pronunciation of the place name, a history of name changes, population, industries, agriculture, climate, and history.

Maps and Atlases

A map is a flat, pictorial representation, usually of the earth's surface or a section of it. There are various types of maps, including astral, physical, historical, and political. An atlas is a collection of maps. An individual map in an atlas may reveal some of the information provided in a gazetteer, but in pictorial, and sometimes tabular, rather than narrative form. Information given in an atlas can range from a simple depiction of a geographic area, with distances and topographic features indicated, to detailed information about such aspects of an area as population, mineral and energy resources, and agriculture. In addition to maps, some atlases offer articles and tables, including information on weather, geology, or zip codes.

Guidebooks

A guidebook generally focuses on a specific country, region, city, or even an individual museum or building, differing from a gazetteer or atlas which includes places from all over the world. A guidebook for the traveler or visitor provides basic information about a specific place. For instance, a guidebook for Rome, Italy might list hotels, restaurants, museums, and other city attractions with which the local resident would be familiar, but the visitor would not.

While each geographic source offers information about places, each has unique qualities most appropriate for answering certain types of place queries. For example, the query, "Which is farther from New York City, Chicago or Philadelphia?" would be best answered using a map because the map scale allows calculation of distances. A gazetteer would include each of these three cities, but would not relate them to each other. Similarly, guidebooks for each city would focus on that city alone, emphasizing basic information needed by visitors only to that area.

DESCRIPTORS FOR GEOGRAPHICAL SOURCES

Given

- Place (4)
- Term–Subject (5)

Wanted

- Date (7)
- Illustration (8)
- Numeric information—measurement (9a)
- Numeric information—counting (9b)
- Person (11)
- Address–Location (12)
- Background information (14c)

Table 4-5 gives a sample gazetteer reference source.

TABLE 4-5
Sample Reference Source: Gazetteer

Title	*Columbia Lippincott Gazetteer of the World*
Coverage	Includes information about cities, states, countries, islands, lakes, mountains, and other geographical features located all over the world.
Organization	Alphabetical by place name.
Given descriptors	Place (4) Term–Subject (5)
Wanted descriptors	Numeric information (9) Address; general location (12) Definition–Symbol (14a) Background information (14c)
SAMPLE QUERY	*How do you pronounce the name of this city in France: Marseilles?*
	ACCESS POINT: Marseilles
	ANSWER: /märsālz'/or/marsā/[a]

[a] From Seltzer, Leon E., (ed.), *Columbia Lippincott Gazetteer of the World.* Morningside Heights, New York: Columbia University Press, 1952. P. 1157.

GUIDES TO THE LITERATURE

A guide to the literature focuses on a specific subject area or discipline, and lists sources of available information related to it. Some guides to the literature are more general, covering many subject areas, such as Sheehy's *Guide to Reference Books.*[2] A guide may include bibliographies, indexing and abstracting sources, periodicals, dictionaries, and subject encyclopedias within a particular discipline, with annotations for each title. Also included may be an introduction to the discipline, techniques of literature searching, and lists of libraries, publishers, and other organizations related to the topic.

Guides to the literature are lead-in tools, as they guide the reference librarian to sources of information on a subject, rather than to the information itself. They can also be useful as selection tools, when building a library collection in the subject field covered. Another use of guides to the literature is in identifying a specific title within a general category of reference tools. If, for example, you determine that the type of tool needed to answer

[2] Sheehy, Eugene P. *A Guide to Reference Books.* Chicago: American Library Association, 1976.

a specific query is a scientific encyclopedia, a guide to the literature of the sciences could be checked to identify the titles of some scientific encyclopedias.

DESCRIPTORS FOR GUIDES TO THE LITERATURE

Given

Term–Subject (5)
Specific publication (6)

Wanted

Organization (10)
Bibliography (13a)
Document verification (13c)
Recommendation (14b)
Background information (14c)

An example of a guide to the literature is included in Chapter 5, p. 54.

HANDBOOKS; MANUALS

Handbooks and manuals are compact reference tools that provide essential information on a specific subject area or discipline in a concise and comprehensive form. They may include compilations of miscellaneous information such as literary, historical, and statistical data on the subjects covered.

Frequently handbooks and manuals are directed more toward the experienced specialist or practitioner with an understanding of a subject and not toward the general lay reader. For example, a scientific handbook, such as a handbook of physics, will give information in narrative format as well as in tables, charts, and graphs that include symbols, formulas, and equations which may prove confusing to the general user.

DESCRIPTORS FOR HANDBOOKS AND MANUALS

Given

Abbreviation–Symbol (1)
Term–Subject (5)

Wanted

Illustration (8)
Numeric information—measurement (9a)
Numeric information—counting (9b)

TABLE 4-6
Sample Reference Source: Manual

Title	*U.S. Government Manual*
Coverage	The official handbook of the Federal government, which provides information on the purposes and programs of most government agencies, lists top level personnel and gives agency addresses and phone numbers.
Organization	Agencies and departments are arranged under the appropriate branch of government. Name, subject, and agency indexes are provided.
Given descriptors	Abbreviation (1) Organization (2) Person (3) Term–Subject (5)
Wanted descriptors	Date (7) Organization (10) Person (11) Address–general location (12) Background information (14c)
SAMPLE QUERY	*Who is the Director of the **Federal Register**?*
	ACCESS POINT: Agency index, under "Federal Register, Office of the," refers to page 551 of the *Manual.*
	ANSWER: The Director of the Office of the Federal Register is Fred J. Emery.[a]

[a] From *1977–1978 U.S. Government Manual.* Washington, D.C.: U.S. Government Printing Office, 1977.

Definition (14a)
Background information (14c)

Table 4-6 gives a sample manual reference source.

INDEXES, BIBLIOGRAPHIES, AND ABSTRACTS

Indexes

An index is a guide to the contents of a source or group of sources of recorded knowledge. The contents an index locates may be items, terms, words, ideas, concepts, or knowledge. Indexing provides access to documents or other means of recorded communication by providing a systematic arrangement of the contents in a different scheme (frequently an alphabetical arrangement) than that used for the material itself. The index provides for each term or concept, etc. to be traced by means of a bibliographic citation or a symbol.

A familiar type of index is the index to the contents of a book. In it, the concepts covered in the book are alphabetically arranged and their location within the book is indicated by a page number (a symbol). Another commonly used index is a library card catalog, which provides author, title, and subject access to the library's collection. In this case, individual items in the collection are located by another symbol, a call number.

Bibliographies

A bibliography is a list of writings or publications, such as books and journal articles, on a given subject or by a given author. In compiling a bibliography, the subject is first defined and then the materials related to that subject are identified. Like an index, a bibliography is arranged in a systematic order (e.g., alphabetically or chronologically), and provides enough information for cited materials to be located, usually by means of a bibliographic citation.

Abstracts

An abstract is an expanded index citation which also provides a brief summary of the essential points of a document. Thus, it not only locates the document by means of a bibliographic citation, as would an index, but goes one step further in briefly describing the material.

Indexes, bibliographies, and abstracts all function as lead-in tools, by identifying sources in which desired information can be found. In addition, each can serve as an answer-providing tool—the index and bibliography being useful for verification and completion of bibliographic information regarding a specific publication, and the abstract serving as a substitute for the material itself if such condensation can provide the information needed.

DESCRIPTORS FOR INDEXES, BIBLIOGRAPHIES, AND ABSTRACTS

Given

Organization (2)
Person (3)

Place (4)
Term–Subject (5)
Specific publication (6)

Wanted

Bibliography (13a)
Document location (13b)
Document verification (13c)
Background information (14c)

Tables 4-7 through 4-9 give sample indexes, bibliography, and abstracts reference sources.

TABLE 4-7
Sample Reference Source: Index

Title	*Library Literature*
Coverage	A subject and author index to the literature of library and information science, including periodicals, books, pamphlets, films, and microfilms. Sample subject headings include: Children's literature Cataloging Book illustration Copyright
Organization	Alphabetical, dictionary arrangement of names and subjects, with cross-references as needed. Provides a bibliographic citation for each item listed. A list of periodicals indexed is included in each issue.
Given descriptors	Organization (2) Person (3) Place (4) Term–Subject (5) Specific publication (6)
Wanted descriptors	Bibliography (13a) Document verification (13c) Background information (14c)
SAMPLE QUERY	*Could you locate an article by Nelsen (or Nelson) that appeared in* ***Wilson Library Bulletin*** *and concerned the kind of language used in children's books?* ACCESS POINTS (in *Library Literature*): "Children's literature—evaluation," or the name "Nelsen" or "Nelson." CITATION: Nelson, Eva, "Overdue: Take the Cuss Words Out of Kid's Books," *Wilson Library Bulletin*(1974): 132–133.[a]

[a] From *Library Literature 1974*. New York: H. W. Wilson 1975. P. 110.

TABLE 4-8
Sample Reference Source: Bibliography

Title	*Bibliography of Library Automation*
Coverage	This is an updating of earlier bibliographies and covers the latter half of 1971, all of 1972, and the first half of 1973. "Coverage in general is limited to North America, although a few foreign citations are included." A complete bibliographic citation is given for each item.
Organization	Items are listed under subject categories, exemplified by Selective Dissemination and Current Awareness, Indexing and Abstracting, etc.
Given descriptors	Term–Subject (5) Specific publication (6)
Wanted descriptors	Bibliography (13a) Document verification (13c) Background information (14c)
SAMPLE QUERY	*Are there any references to aspects of interlibrary loan operations?* ACCESS POINT: *Interlibrary Loan*, p. 173 ANSWER: Scholz, William H. *Intrasystem Loans at Timberland Regional Library: A Study and Computer Simulation. Olympia.* Washington: Washington State Library, 1972. Stevens, Rolland E. *A Feasibility Study of Centralized and Regionalized Interlibrary Loan Centres.* Washington, D.C.: Association of Research Libraries, 1973, 65 pp. ED 076 206.[a]

[a] West, Martha W. (Comp.) *Bibliography of Library Automation.* Chicago: American Library Association, 1975. P. 173.

MONOGRAPH; TEXT

Monographs and texts are treatises on a subject or class of subjects, usually detailed but not extremely specialized in scope. The book you are now reading falls into the monograph or text category.

A monograph or text is not considered a "reference book" in the traditional sense of the term, as it is not intended for quick referral but rather to be read completely. However, although they are not a traditional reference source, monographs and texts contain a wealth of information useful in answering reference queries. In addition to a detailed discussion of a subject, these sources often contain extensive bibliographies, as well as illustrations, charts, and tables (when appropriate to the topic being covered).

A monograph or text may be written in a style understandable to a nonspecialist, or may be aimed at the reader who already has a basic understanding of the topic. For example, a patron request for a general description or for a particular fact related to photosynthesis could frequently be satisfied by a monograph or text. In it one would probably find a more detailed dis-

TABLE 4-9
Sample Reference Source: Abstracts

Title	*Resources in Education*
Coverage	A monthly abstract journal announcing recent report literature related to the field of education.
Organization	Each document surogate listed in *Resources in Education* consists of its bibliographic citation, abstract, cost, and list of indexing terms. Document surrogates are arranged by subject categories, such as Career Education, Educational Management, Information Resources, Junior Colleges, etc. Each monthly issue contains indexes to subjects, authors, institutions, and clearinghouse numbers. The indexes are cumulated semiannually. Indexes to *Resources in Education* are also searchable on-line by computers, as will be illustrated in Chapter 10.
Given descriptors	Organization (2) Person (3) Term–Subject (5)
Wanted descriptors	Date (7) Bibliography (13a) Document location (13b) Document verification (13c) Background information (14c)
SAMPLE QUERY	*Is there a report issued in 1977 by the Georgia Institute of Technology on Semiotics?* ACCESS POINT: *Institutions Index* (July–December, 1977), p. 721. Georgia Institute of Technology, ED 138 304. ANSWER: ED 138 304IR 004 747. Pearson, Charls, Slamecka, Vladimir. *Semiotic Foundations of Information Science. Final Project Report.* Georgia Institute of Technology, Atlanta. School of Information and Computer Science, 1977. EDRS. Price of microfilm $0.83; hard cover, $3.50 plus postage.[a]

[a] From *Resources in Education. 1956–* . Monthly. Washington D.C.: U.S. Department of Health, Education, and Welfare. National Institute of Education (1977) 12:116.

cussion than provided in a dictionary or encyclopedia, but a more general approach than presented in a primary publication (see p. 44 ff. for a discussion of primary publications). (Monographs and texts differ from primary publications in another respect, in that they frequently contain edited or modified results of original research or scholarship.)

DESCRIPTORS FOR MONOGRAPHS AND TEXTS

Given

Organization (2)
Person (3)

Place (4)
Term–Subject (5)

Wanted

Date (7)
Illustration (8)
Organization (10)
Person (11)
Address–Location (12)
Bibliography (13a)
Definition–Symbol (14a)
Background information (14c)

Table 4-10 gives a sample monograph reference source.

TABLE 4-10
Sample Reference Source: Monograph

Title	*Resume Writing: A Comprehensive How-to-Do-It Guide*
Coverage	The purpose of the book is to provide aid in the preparation of resumés. It includes information on the purpose of resumés, techniques for writing successful resumés, and suggestions for their reproduction and distribution. Various resumé styles are described, with examples.
Organization	Topics are presented in sections arranged according to steps in resumé preparation from start to finish. An index is included.
Given descriptors	Term–Subject (5)
Wanted descriptors	Background information (14c)
SAMPLE QUERY	*What is a "Harvard" resumé and what does it look like?*
	ACCESS POINT: Harvard résumé (in index and table of contents).
	ANSWER: The Harvard résumé is a style of resumé associated with the Harvard Graduate School of Business Administration. It has narrow margins and long paragraphs. Examples are given in the text.[a]

[a] From Bostwick, Burdette E. *Resume Writing: A Comprehensive How-to-Do-It Guide.* New York: Wiley, 1976. Pp. 71–75.

PRIMARY PUBLICATIONS

A primary publication is an original unpublished paper or a published report of research or scholarship, usually in its initial, unedited form. And it is usually the first print appearance of research and scholarship by an individual or group. Because it has not been condensed or interpreted by any outside individual, it provides information from the source.

Primary publications are frequently the result of experiments or surveys, and may be published as articles in primary journals, or as conference proceedings, individually published or unpublished distributed reports, or unpublished dissertations. A primary publication concerned with photosynthesis would not aim primarily to provide a definition and background information on the concept, but would most likely present innovative research and analysis concerning the process. Therefore, the primary publication would be best suited not for the individual seeking a basic understanding of photosynthesis, but for the person who already understands the process and seeks further research and analysis on the topic.

DESCRIPTORS FOR PRIMARY PUBLICATIONS

Given

- Organization (2)
- Person (3)
- Term–Subject (5)

Wanted

- Illustration (8)
- Numeric information—measurement (9a)
- Numeric information—counting (9b)
- Bibliography (13a)
- Background information (14c)

Table 4-11 gives a sample primary publication reference source.

NONBIOGRAPHICAL DIRECTORIES

Nonbiographical directories are, as you would guess, directories which do not emphasize facts about people. Instead, they have been compiled to provide information about organizations, agencies, firms, clubs, societies, associations, institutions, or official bodies. These directories may also focus on manufacturers or business houses in a particular trade, profession, or region.

The information frequently given about such organizations includes their address, structure, and operations. Although nonbiographical in emphasis, these directories often include information about people, such as names of officers or lists of members. The approach differs from that of biographical directories, however, in that the access point is usually not the individual's name, but the function or position held by that individual in the

TABLE 4-11
Sample Reference Source: Primary Publication

Title	*Journal of the American Chemical Society*
Coverage	"The *Journal of the American Chemical Society* is devoted to the publication of research papers in all fields of chemistry. . . . Articles most appropriate for publication in the *Journal* are those which deal with some phase of 'pure' chemistry as distinguished from 'applied' chemistry."
Organization	The individual biweekly issues contain full-length articles, communications to the editor, book reviews, and advertisements. There are annual author and subject (keyword-from-title) indexes.
Given descriptors	Organization (2) Person (3) Term–Subject (5)
Wanted descriptors	Illustration (8) Numeric information—measurement (9a) Numeric information—counting (9b) Bibliography (13a) Background information (14c)
SAMPLE QUERY	*Does the* ***Journal of the American Chemical Society*** *give any instructions to authors on submitting manuscripts?* ANSWER: Instructions to contributors are listed in the first issue of each volume.[a]

[a] From the *Journal of the American Chemical Society*, 1879– . Biweekly.

organization. These directories are usually arranged in either classed or alphabetical order.

DESCRIPTORS FOR NONBIOGRAPHICAL DIRECTORIES

Given

- Organization (2)
- Place (4)
- Term–subject (5)

Wanted

- Date (7)
- Numeric information—counting (9b)
- Organization (10)
- Person (11)
- Address–Location (12)
- Background information (14c)

Table 4-12 gives a sample directory reference source.

TABLE 4-12
Sample Reference Source: Directory

Title	*American Library Directory*
Coverage	Libraries in the U.S. and Canada are listed with directory information given, including: address; telephone number; holdings; circulation; personnel; and heads of departments.
Organization	Libraries in the U.S. are arranged according to the state and city where they are located.
Given descriptors	Organization (2) Place (4)
Wanted descriptors	Numeric information—counting (9b) Organization (10) Person (11) Address–Location (12) Background information (14c)
SAMPLE QUERY	*What is the name and mailing address of the public library in Bloomington, Indiana?* ACCESS POINT: Indiana, Bloomington ANSWER: Monroe Country Public Library 303 E. Kirkwood Avenue Bloomington, Indiana 47401.[a]

[a] From *American Library Directory*, 29th edition. New York: Bowker, 1974. P. 278.

YEARBOOKS; ALMANACS

The most outstanding characteristic of both yearbooks and almanacs is their currency, as they are typically published on an annual basis. Retrospective editions can be used to locate information about past events, and in the study of trends and developments.

The scope of yearbooks and almanacs may be general, or limited to a specific field. General yearbooks are frequently published as supplements to general encyclopedias, and contain information in a format similar to that found in general encyclopedias. Specialized yearbooks contain information related to specific disciplines. Almanacs contain current information in both descriptive and statistical form. A general purpose almanac may include information concerning almost any field of human knowledge and endeavor. This information is presented concisely, and frequently in a tabular format.

DESCRIPTORS FOR YEARBOOKS AND ALMANACS

Given

Organization (2)
Person (3)

Place (4)
Term–Subject (5)

Wanted.

Date (7)
Illustration (8)
Numeric information—measurement (9a)

TABLE 4-13
Sample Reference Source: Almanac

Title	*World Almanac and Book of Facts*
Coverage	Brief, general information in many areas of interest. Information is presented in charts, tables, maps illustrations, graphs, and textual material. Some of the types of information included are: Olympic games records Weights and measures Monthly temperatures in the U.S. Mayors and city managers in large U.S. and Canadian cities
Organization	Loose subject arrangement, with individual topics grouped within larger categories such as: Education Environment Sports Includes a general index and a quick reference index.
Given descriptors	Abbreviation–Symbol (1) Organization (2) Person (3) Place (4) Term–Subject (5)
Wanted descriptors	Date (7) Numeric information—measurement (9a) Numeric information—counting (9b) Organization (10) Person (11) Address–Location (12) Background information (14c)
SAMPLE QUERY	*What is the tallest building in the U.S.?* ACCESS POINT: United States, Superlative United States Statistics ANSWER: The tallest building in the U.S. is the Sears Tower in Chicago, which is 1454 feet high.[a]

[a] From *World Almanac and Book of Facts*. New York: Newspaper Enterprise Association, 1976. P. 150.

Numeric information—counting (9b)
Organization (10)
Address–Location (12)
Bibliography (13a)
Document location (13b)
Background information (14c)

Table 4-13 and 4-14 give a sample almanac and yearbook reference source.

TABLE 4-14
Sample Reference Source: Yearbook

Title	*The ALA Yearbook*
Coverage	Summarizes library-related events and activities during the past year, including concise state-of-the-art reviews for library-related topics, information concerning ALA and other organizations concerned with libraries, as well as biographical data for outstanding librarians.
Organization	The majority of the articles are presented in an encyclopedic arrangement, alphabetically by topical subject headings. An index provides access to information included in the yearbook by means of subject, name, and title headings.
Given descriptors	Organization (2) Person (3) Place (4) Term–Subject (5)
Wanted descriptors	Date (7) Numeric information—counting (9b) Organization (10) Person (11) Bibliography (13a) Background information (14c)
SAMPLE QUERY	*What is the Council on Library Technical Assistants?* ACCESS POINT: Council on Library Technical Assistants ANSWER: The Council (COLT) is an international association of individuals and organizations involved in the training of library–media assistants and other paraprofessionals.[a]

[a] From Duvall, Betty. "Council on Library Technical Assistants." *The ALA Yearbook: A Review of Library Events 1975*. Chicago: American Library Association, 1976. Pp. 148–149.

SUMMARY

This chapter has provided an introduction to several categories of reference tools. Individual titles within each category tend to contain similar types of information, and in an attempt to summarize the information content of each group, descriptors have been listed. Of course, individual titles within a group will differ in their information content, and may contain additional information or less information than represented by the descriptors listed for a typical title in that group. In the exercises that follow, you will have an opportunity to examine specific titles within several categories and summarize their contents using descriptors.

QUESTIONS FOR DISCUSSION

Can you think of a specific reference tool that has the words "dictionary" or "encyclopedia" in its title, but that actually belongs in another tool category?

How might the information given about photography differ in a dictionary, an encyclopedia, a primary source, or monograph–text?

Which categories of tools might be best suited for use by a specialist in a topic? By a novice in a topic?

Can you think of any specific reference titles that do not fit into any of the tool categories discussed in this chapter?

EXERCISE Categories of Answer-Providing Tools

(Select one title from each of the four categories of tools given below—or identify any other title within the category—and select given and wanted descriptors that describe the contents of that title.)

1. Biographical Sources
   American Men and Women of Science
   Dictionary of American Biography
   The New York Times Obituaries Index
   Official Congressional Directory
   Webster's Biographical Dictionary
2. Dictionaries
   Acronyms and Initialisms Dictionary
   Cassell's New French Dictionary
   NBC Handbook of Pronunciation
   Oxford English Dictionary
   Webster's New Dictionary of Synonyms
3. Nonbiographical Directories
   Guide to American Directories
   Encyclopedia of Associations

The Foundation Directory
Poor's Register of Corporations, Directors, and Executives
Thomas' Register of American Manufacturers

4. Guides to the Literature
   Borchardt, *How to Find Out in Philosophy and Psychology*
   Rogers, *The Humanities; A Selective Guide to Information Sources*
   Walford, *Guide to Reference Material*
   White, *Sources of Information in the Social Sciences*
   Wynar, *Guide to Reference Books for School Media Centers*

5

Lead-In Tools

In the preceding chapter, we described different types of answer-providing tools in terms of their information content. This knowledge alone, however, is not sufficient for answering specific reference queries. To do this we must progress from selection of the type of answer-providing tool likely to have an answer, for example, an encyclopedia, to a specific title within that category, for example the *Encyclopedia Britannica*. There are several additional steps that must be completed before a reference query can be answered, but in this chapter we will restrict our attention to selecting a specific title after determining the general type of answer-providing tool likely to satisfy the query.

Generally, the practicing reference librarian follows one of two paths when selecting a specific title from a category of answer-providing tools. If similar queries have occurred before, a particular title may come immediately to mind. For example, if the home office address of the Dow Chemical Company, a well-known U.S. chemical manufacturer, is requested, a reference librarian would probably go directly to the latest edition of the *Thomas Register of Manufacturers*, a directory that contains the answer to this query. The translation from type of tool, directory, to a specific tool, the *Thomas Register of Manufacturers*, was made in the librarian's head. He or she identified this as a directory query and was familiar with a specific directory containing information about manufacturers.

If the query is a unique one, however, the librarian may not be able to recall a specific title within a category of tools without referring to a lead-in tool to direct him or her to sources of information on the topic. In the case of a patron request for a Serbo-Croatian–English dictionary, for example, the librarian knows the type of tool needed, a dictionary, but may not be able to think of a specific title. As there are literally thousands of dictionaries, it is impossible for a librarian to remember all of their titles. In fact, it is unnecessary to do so because reference tools, called "lead-in tools," have been developed to aid in identifying specific titles.

As their name indicates, lead-in tools lead the librarian from a general category of tools to a specific title within that category. They identify sources in which information can be found, rather than provide the information itself. Lead-in tools thus serve as a bridge between the type of answer-providing tool and a specific answer-providing tool. In the preceding example, the request for a Serbo-Croatian–English dictionary, there are two specific lead-in tools we will describe (see Tables 5-1 and 5-2), a guide to the literature and a bibliography of a type of tool.

Let us now demonstrate how we can satisfy our example request for a Serbo-Croatian–English dictionary through use of the card catalog, Sheehy's *Guide to Reference Books*, and Brewer's *Dictionaries, Encyclopedias, and Other World-Related Books 1966–1974* (Detroit: Gale Research Co.: 1975). In the card catalog of a large university library, we found the heading "Dictionaries" contained a *see* reference to "Encyclopedias and Dictionaries." Under the potential access point, "Encyclopedias and Dictionaries—Serbo-Croatian," there was no listing. (This is because under the Library of Congress system for subject headings in use at the library, encyclopedias and dictionaries of a particular subject are under the subject itself with a subdivision, "Dictionaries." Therefore, before searching, it is a good idea to check classification rules for the system in use at a particular library, whether Library of Congress or other.) It was then necessary to turn to the access point in the card catalog "Serbo-Croatian Language—Dictionaries—English." This step yielded the following title: "Benson, Morton. *Serbo-Croatian—English Dictionary*. Philadelphia: University of Pennsylvania, 1971."

In Sheehy's *Guide to Reference Books*, the access point used was "AD—Language Dictionaries." Included under the subheading "Foreign Languages" was Item AD617: "Benson, Morton, *Serbo-Croatian—English Dictionary*. Philadelphia: University of Pennsylvania, 1971."

TABLE 5-1
Sample Lead-in Tool: Guide to the Literature

Author	Eugene P. Sheehy (Ed.)
Title	*Guide to Reference Books.* 9th ed. Chicago: American Library Association, 1976.
Coverage	A guide to reference books covering all subject fields. It is intended for use with large research library collections, but also for smaller collections.
Organization	This ninth edition is basically similar to the previous eighth. There are five broad sections, each designated by a letter of the alphabet: "A—General Reference Works"; "B—The Humanities"; "C—Social Sciences"; "D—History and Area Studies"; and "E—Pure and Applied Sciences." These broad categories are further broken down into subsections, which are further divided into subdivisions. For example, "Humanities" (Section B) includes a subheading for "Religion" (BB), which is further broken down according to types of religions: "Hinduism, Islam, Shintoism," etc. Each item is given a specific identification code. Thus under "Islam," for example, we find "BB342": Geddes, Charles L. *An Analytical Guide to the Bibliographies of Islam, Muhammad, and the Qu'ran.* Each item is given its full bibliographic citation and is briefly annotated. The combination of a two-letter code plus number is unique to each listing in Sheehy's *Guide*. The *Guide*'s index includes author and subject entries and most, but not all, title entries. Throughout, the *Guide*'s emphasis is on tools for scholarly research, although a wider range of popular reference works meeting standards of usefulness and reliability has also been included. An important feature of the *Guide* is the reprint (pp. xiii–xv) of Isadore Gilbert Mudge's essay, "Reference Department," reprinted from the sixth edition. It remains a classic description of reference work.
Given descriptors	Abbreviation (1) Organization (2) Person (3) Place (4) Term–Subject (5) Specific publication (6)
Wanted descriptors	Bibliography (13a) Recommendation (14b)
SAMPLE QUERY	*Is there a journal of book reviews that covers books on architecture?* ACCESS POINT: (Index). Book review indexes, pp. 36–37. Book Review Indexes ANSWER-PROVIDING TOOL: A414 *Index to Book Reviews in the Humanities, 1960.* Detroit: Phillip Thomson, 1960. In annotation; includes architecture.

TABLE 5-2
Sample Lead-in Tool: Bibliography of a Type of Tool

Author	Annie Brewer (Ed.)
Title	*Dictionaries, Encyclopedias, and other Word-Related Books 1966–1974.* Detroit: Gale Research Co., 1975.
Coverage	From very general to very specific, including dictionaries, encyclopedias, concordances, ABCs, word books, glossaries, vocabularies, topical indexes, lexicons, gazetteers, and thesauri. The material encompassed in these works includes not only terms and phrases and general vocabulary in all languages, but also acronyms, Americanisms, colloquialisms, etymologies, glossaries, idioms and expressions, orthography, provincialisms, and slang. Coverage is of titles appearing from 1966 through 1974.
Organization	Hierarchical, by Library of Congress classification, with the exception of Law (K) which is filed alphabetically by main entry. The broad categories given include General Works (A), Philosophy (B–BJ), Religion (BL–BX), History (C and D), Geography (G), Social Science (H), Political Science (J), Law (K), Education (L), Music (M), The Arts (N), Language and Literature (P), Pure Science (Q), Medicine (R), Agriculture (S), Technology (T), Military Science (U and V), and Bibliography and Library Science (Z). Subdivision is also by letter, for example: under General Works (A), AZ refers to Signs and Symbols; under Geography (G), GA refers to Cartography, etc; under Philosophy (B–BJ), BH refers to Aesthetics. Each page of the book consists of columns of reproduced Library of Congress cards. There are no annotations. No author or title indexes are provided, though the table of contents is followed by a key word index that lists items by subject area and page.
Given descriptors	Abbreviation (1) Term–Subject (5)
Wanted descriptors	Bibliography (13a)
SAMPLE QUERY	*I need information about some terms used in the folk tales of the Australian aborigines.* ACCESS POINT: (Table of Contents): G—Geography; (Subheading): GR—Folklore, pp. 109–110. ANSWER-PROVIDING TOOL: P. 110. Wannan, Bill (Comp.). *Australian Folklore: A Dictionary of Lore, Legends, and Popular Allusions.* Melbourne, Australia: Lansdowne, 1970.

In Brewer's *Dictionaries*, the access point used was Category P, "Language and Literature," which included PG— "Slavic, Balto-Slavic, and Albanian Languages." Here again the listing found was for "Benson, Morton. *Serbo-Croatian–English Dictionary*. Philadelphia: University of Pennsylvania, 1971."

BASIS FOR SELECTING LEAD-IN TOOLS

Typically, when a lead-in tool needs to be consulted in order to identify a specific answer-providing tool, the reference librarian has a choice to make. As we have seen, he or she can use the card catalog, a guide to the literature, and, in some cases, a bibliography of a specific type of answer-providing tool. When several alternative types of lead-in tools are available, the librarian must decide which to consult first. No definite sequence can be identified, but a discussion of the characteristics of lead-in tools will help in establishing guidelines for an efficient search sequence.

An ideal lead-in tool would have the following characteristics:

1. Inclusion of all potentially useful answer-providing tools
2. Provision of a basis for evaluating the usefulness of individual titles listed
3. Indication of the location of answer-providing titles in the library collection
4. Ease of access within the lead-in tool, providing for efficient identification of potentially useful answer-providing titles

The Card Catalog

None of the three types of lead-in tools deserves a high rating for each of the preceding characteristics. The card catalog includes potentially useful answer-providing titles only when they are in the library collection and have been cataloged. Thus a journal article or a section of a handbook is not likely to be identified through the card catalog because a part of a journal or handbook would not have been cataloged. The card catalog entry furnishes a bibliographic description of the item, including indication of whether it contains a bibliography and/or illustrations, as well as subject headings which describe the title (as tracings in the main entry). There is, however, no evaluation of the tool as would be found in a book review. The entry also shows the location of the item in the library collection by means of the call number. Access in a card catalog search for a specific title would be by subject heading, which may or may not be easy to determine.

Guides to the Literature

Guides to the literature may include answer-providing tools that are not likely to be listed in the card catalog, such as journal articles or sections of handbooks. In many cases, guides provide more in-depth descriptions than other lead-in tools (e.g., the number of terms included in a dictionary), as well as providing evaluative comments. These features are useful in selecting specific answer-providing titles. The library location is usually not listed in the guide unless the librarian has written in this information. In some cases, as for example in Sheehy's *Guide to Reference Books*, the Library of Congress class number is given. The approximate location can be obtained through use of Sheehy in libraries using this classification system. Otherwise, a second step, a search in the card catalog under the author or title of the tool identified in the guide, would be required. Access to titles included in guides may be by means of a subject index and/or by a subject-classified arrangement of the listed items. As with subject headings in the card catalog, this approach may or may not be easy to use.

Bibliographies of Types of Tools

The characteristic of bibliographies—focusing on a single type of tool—resembles that of guides. Bibliographic items are typically described more fully than in the card catalog, although in our example, Brewer, the format is exactly that of catalog cards. Evaluative statements are sometimes given. Bibliographies of single types of tools are likely to be more comprehensive than corresponding sections of guides to the literature, and this is the primary advantage of this type of lead-in tool. The library location of the title identified has to be checked in the card catalog. Access to the included item may be by subject heading and/or by subject classification.

CHOOSING A LEAD-IN TOOL

Based on the characteristics of lead-in tools, it is suggested that the card catalog be searched first if the answer-providing tool is likely to be a cataloged item, and if the title selected will not require any evaluation prior to use. Using the card catalog allows immediate, one-step identification of the location of the title; for most guides to the literature or bibliographies of types of tools, a secondary step is required. If the answer-providing tool is likely to be an uncataloged item or if there is a choice to be made between a large number of titles, either a guide to the literature or a bibliography of a type of tool should be consulted first. When a choice between a guide to the literature and a bibliography of a type of tool is available, a decision is likely to depend on the recency of each source and on the amount of information given for individually listed items in each source.

SUMMARY

In this chapter we have discussed the need for and use of lead-in tools. Lead-in tools are used to identify the title of a specific answer-providing tool after the type of tool needed to answer a query has been determined. And lead-in tools are essential for answering many reference queries. (At the end of this chapter, we provide an exercise in the use of the card catalog, guides to the literature, and bibliographies of specific types of answer-providing tools. In this exercise, you will need to select a lead-in tool with which to identify the title of a specific answer-providing tool that may contain an answer to the query.)

QUESTIONS FOR DISCUSSION

Indicate types of queries for which lead-in tools would be needed before identifying an answer-providing tool, and those for which lead-in tools would not be needed.

How much information about specific answer-providing titles may be provided in a lead-in tool?

How can one evaluate the adequacy of lead-in tools?

Give examples of queries for which the lead-in tools listed in this chapter could be used as answer-providing tools.

If you were asked to conduct a study aimed at determining the least search sequence (the fastest way of identifying) an answer-providing title with the aid of lead-in tools, how would you go about doing this?

EXERCISE Lead-In Tools

(For each of the following queries, use a lead-in tool to identify the citation of a likely answer-providing title that would satisfy the query. You may use lead-in tools from the list below, or identify other lead-in tools on your own. Keep a record of the access point used to locate information in the lead-in tool, as well as the page number in the lead-in tool where the answer-providing title was listed.)

Rogers, A. Robert. *The Humanities: A Selective Guide to Information Sources.* Littleton, Colo.: Libraries Unlimited, 1974.

Sheehy, Eugene P. *Guide to Reference Books.* 9th ed. Chicago: American Library Association, 1976.

Walford, A. J. *Guide to Reference Materials.* 3rd ed. London: Library Association, 1973.

White, Carl M. and Associates. *Sources of information in the Social Sciences: A Guide to the Literature.* 2nd ed. Chicago: American Library Association, 1973.

SAMPLE QUERY: *I need a guide to the social history of Chicanos in the United States.*

ANSWER TO SAMPLE QUERY:

1. *Answer-providing title*: Stanford University, Center for Latin-American Studies. *The Mexican-American: A Selected and Annotated Bibliography.* 2nd ed. Edited by Luis G. Nogales. Stanford, Calif.: The Center, 1977.
2. *Lead-in tool*: White, *Sources of Information in the Social Sciences.*
3. *Page number in lead-in tool*: P. 277.
4. *Access point*: Index. Number E 234. Mexican American.

Queries

1. "I want to find out about the Cobra movement in European painting about 10 years ago."
2. "Were any newspapers published in the Leeward Islands during the sixteenth century?"
3. "How many kinds of monks were there in the Church of England 10 years after World War II?"
4. "How long does it take to perform Beethoven's Fifth Symphony?"
5. "What is the average temperature in August in Lhasa, Tibet?"
6. "Where can I find a picture of Rodin's sculpture, 'Citizens of Calais?'"
7. "How long ago did humans first live in Norfolk, England?"
8. "What was the worst earthquake in U.S. history?"
9. "What types of clothes were worn by the ancient Egyptians?"
10. "Where did the Mascouten Indians of North America live around A.D. 1500?"
11. "When was Lord Attleborough the British Governor of Virginia?"
12. "I need a nontechnical explanation of the ideas of Martin Luther."
13. "Was Stetson University in Florida accredited in 1965?"

ANSWERS TO EXERCISE

1

a. *Answer-Providing Title*: *Phaidon Dictionary of Twentieth Century Art.* New York: Phaidon, 1973. Distributed by Praeger.

b. *Lead-In Tool*: Rogers, *The Humanities.*
c. *Page Number in Lead-In Tool*: P. 147; number 305.
d. *Access Point*: Rogers (Subject index). Art, *see also* Visual arts. (Visual arts: Dictionaries, 145–147; Encyclopedias, 145–147.)

2

a. *Answer-Providing Title:* Baker, E. C. *A Guide to Records in the Leeward Islands.* Oxford, England: published for the University of the West Indies by Blackwell, 1965.
b. *Lead-In Tool*: Walford, *Guide to Reference Materials.*
c. *Page Number in Lead-In Tool*: P. 469; number 972.97.
d. *Access Point*: Walford (Index). West Indies, History, P. 469.

3

a. *Answer-Providing Title*: Church of England. Advisory Council on Religious Communities. *Guide to Religious Communities of the Anglican Communion.* London, Mowbray, 1955. New edition.

or

Anson, P. F. *The Call of the Cloister: Religious Communities and Kindred Bodies in the Anglican Communion.* London: Society for the Promotion of Christian Knowledge, 1955.
b. *Lead-In Tool*: Walford, *Guide to Reference Materials.*
c. *Page Number in Lead-In Tool*: P. 43; number 271.283. (Both)
d. *Access Point*: Walford (Index). Religious orders, pp. 42–43.

4

a. *Answer-Providing Title*: Aronowsky, Salomon. *Performing Times of Orchestral Works.* London: Bean, 1959.
b. *Lead-In Tool*: Rogers, *The Humanities.*
c. *Page Number in Lead-In Tool*: P. 211; number 565.
d. *Access Point*: Rogers (Subject index). Music bibliographies, pp. 211–215.

5

a. *Answer-Providing Title*: Conway, H., May, S., and Armstrong, E. *The Weather Handbook.* Atlanta: Conway, 1965.
b. *Lead-In Tool*: Sheehy, *Guide to Reference Books.*
c. *Page Number in Lead-In Tool*: P. 752; number EE 124.
d. *Access Point*: Climatology EE 122-EE 128.

6

a. *Answer-Providing Title*: Clapp, Jane. *Sculpture Index.* Metuchen, N. J.: Scarecrow, 1970–1971. 2 volumes. Volume 1: *Sculpture of Europe and the Contemporary Middle East.*
b. *Lead-In Tool*: Rogers, *The Humanities.*
c. *Page Number in Lead-In Tool*: P. 175; number 491.
d. *Access Point*: Rogers (Subject index). Sculpture, pp. 133, 175–177.

7

a. *Answer-Providing Title*: *The Victoria History of the County of Norfolk.* London: Constable, 1901–1906. Volumes. 1–2.
b. *Lead-In Tool*: Walford, *Guide to Reference Materials.*
c. *Page Number in Lead-In Tool*: P. 446; number 942.61 (02).
d. *Access Point*: Walford (Index). Norfolk, history—pp. 445–446.

8

a. *Answer-Providing Title*: U.S. Coast and Geodetic Survey. *Earthquake History of the United States*. Rev. ed. (through 1963). Washington, D.C.: U.S. Government Printing Office, 1965–1966.
b. *Lead-In Tool*: Sheehy, *Guide to Reference Books*.
c. *Page Number in Lead-In Tool*: P. 758; number EE 202.
d. *Access Point*: Seismology EE 201-EE 203.

9

a. *Answer-Providing Title*: Payne, Blanche. *History of Costume, from the Ancient Egyptians to the Twentieth Century*. New York: Harper, 1965.
b. *Lead-In Tool*: Sheehy, *Guide to Reference Books*.
c. *Page Number in Lead-In Tool*: P. 396; number BF 47.
d. *Access Point*: Costume—History and illustration, BF 36-BF 52.

10

a. *Answer-Providing Title*: Driver, Harold E., *etal*., *Indian Tribes of North America*. Baltimore: Waverly, 1953. Also, *Indiana University Publications in Anthropology and Linguistics*, Memoir 9.
b. *Lead-In Tool*: White, *Sources of Information in the Social Sciences*.
c. *Page Number in Lead-in Tool*: P. 369; number F 523.
d. *Access Point*: White (Index). Anthropology, atlases and maps, F 518-F 528.

11

a. *Answer-Providing Title*: Henige, David P. *Colonial Governors from the Fifteenth Century to the Present: A Comprehensive List*. Madison, Wisconsin: University of Wisconsin Press, 1970.
b. *Lead-In Tool*: White, *Sources of Information in the Social Sciences*.
c. *Page Number in Lead-In Tool*: P. 542; number I 500.
d. *Access Point*: White (Index). Colonial governors from the fifteenth century to the present.

12

a. *Answer-Providing Title*: Hughes, Philip. *A Popular History of the Reformation*. Garden City, N.Y.: Doubleday, 1957.
b. *Lead-In Tool*: White, *Sources of Information in the Social Sciences*.
c. *Page Number in Lead-In Tool*: P. 93; B 82.
d. *Access Point*: Reformation (History). B 65; B 80–B 88.

13

a. *Answer-Providing Title*: American Council on Education. *Accredited Institutions of Higher Education 1964–*. Washington, D.C.: The Council Annual.
b. *Lead-In Tool*: White, *Sources of Information in the Social Sciences*.
c. *Page Number in Lead-In Tool*: P. 470; number H 513.
d. *Access Point*: Accredited Institutions of Higher Education. H 513.

6

Selection of Search Headings

To locate the page or pages that contain the answer in an answer-providing title, or to locate the page in a lead-in tool on which a specific answer-providing title is listed, three approaches can be used: (*a*) searching the index, (*b*) searching the table of contents, or (*c*) skimming every page of the book. The third approach, skimming every page of the book, is, of course, not an efficient method and would only be used when all else failed. The second approach, searching the table of contents, typically leads you to sections of a book likely to contain the answer, rather than to a specific page. This might be considered the alternate approach to be used when the title being searched contains no index or when the index fails to direct you to the page containing an answer. The first and best approach to use when seeking information in a specific title is typically a search of the index.

THE INDEX

An index is a systematic guide to the contents of a single document, such as a book, or to a collection of documents, such as journal articles. An index can be in any of several formats, including book, card, or machine-readable formats. Indexes vary in several ways and provide differing amounts of information.

An example of an index with which you are familiar is the index in the back (or sometimes the front) of a book. Such an index typically consists of an alphabetically arranged list of single words or phrases and is called an alphabetic subject index. Each item in the index is either an entry or a cross-reference. Each entry consists of a single word or phrase (the heading) followed by the page number(s) in the book on which the topic is discussed (the page reference). Cross-references lead either from terms not used as index headings to those used (e.g., Clemens, Samuel, *see* Twain, Mark), or to related headings for additional information of interest (e.g., Books, 132, *see also* Pamphlets). The types of index headings included in an index vary. Typically, an index will provide access by author and subject. There could also be access by time period, chemical structures, or other access points useful for a particular discipline.

In indexes to collections of documents, such as for journal articles, varying amounts of information may be provided. The fullest possible entry would provide a complete bibliographic citation for each indexed document, including its complete title. A minimal entry would provide a unique number, the accession number, for each document. Also, indexes may be issued at different intervals and may also be cumulated at varying intervals. Some may, for example, be issued monthly and cumulated yearly. Rules for alphabetizing may vary. Author and subject entries may be interfiled or listed separately. Finally, some indexes have elements of vocabulary control (for example, *see* and *see also* cross-references) while others do not. (For these reasons, it is best to read the introduction to the index in order to become familiar with the rules of, and instructions for, using a given index.)

OTHER TYPES OF INDEXES

Keyword-from-Title Index

The keyword-from-title index is so named because it lists document titles rather than subject headings. Such indexes are usually prepared by computer—the listing of titles and arrangement by keywords is a task well-suited for machine compilation.

An example of one form of keyword-from-title index, the keyword-in-context index (KWIC) is illustrated as Figure 6-1. For each document indexed, the title words, complete bibliographic citation, and a unique accession number are put into machine-readable form. In some KWIC indexes,

xperimental chemotherapy of	Guerin tumor.= +rat organs during e	BIOFAI-0022-0656
ascular beta receptors in the	guinea pig and rabbit.= +y and cardiov	JPETAB-0202-0337
yl nucleotide binding sites in	guinea pig heart sarcolemma.= +guan	IJBOBV-0008-0591
n release in isolated perfused	guinea pig hearts.= +on prostaglandi	PRGLBA-0014-0173
le role of prostaglandins in	guinea pig isolated ileum contractions to	PRGLBA-0014-0119
mutagenic intermediates by	guinea pig kidney microsomal enzymes f	TXAPA9-0041-0119
ydroxylation of estrogens by	guinea pig liver slices.= +nce for 16β-h	CJBIAE-0055-0769
-S-ep oxide transferase from	guinea pig liver.= +ties of glutathione	JOBIAO-0082-0407
g subcellular fractions from	guinea pig neocortical tissues, on incuba	JONRA9-0029-0077
ight of subunits and amino+	Guinea pig thyro globulin: molecular we	BBRCA9-0077-0874
iveness of the rabbit and the	guinea pig to probenecid.= +-respons	JPETAB-0202-0466
temperature in the newborn	guinea pig.= +nor adrenaline on body	EXPEAM-0033-1083
eradish per oxidase in the	guinea pig.= Vascular reactions to hors	HCMYAL-0053-0217
hythmias in cats, rabbits and	guinea pigs.= +id on experimental arr	PRGLBA-0014-0163
chole lithiasis in	guinea pigs.= Hypovitaminosis C and	BBRCA9-0077-1030
nd cyclic AMP level of left	guinea-pig atria at different rates of bea	NSAPCC-0299-0009
rnal acetyl cholin esterase in	guinea-pig iris.= +operties of the exte	JONRA9-0029-0151
mechanical responses in the	guinea-pig papillary muscle partially de	NSAPCC-0299-0001
w pi perine amide from Piper	guineense.= +thesis of wisanine, a ne	PYTCAS-0016-1437
2,3,3,3-ennea carbonyl-trian	gulo-tri rhenate(2-).= +-oxo-1,1,1,2,2,	JCDTBI-1977-1667
rinking magnesite-chromite	gunite mass containing additives of sodi	OGNPA2-77-08-040
procedure for calcareous and	gypsiferous soils.= +capacity: a new	SSSJD4-0041-0524
of the α-hemi hydrate into	gypsum transformation in phosphoric ac	PRCHAB-0056-0318

ence of calcium chloride and	gypsum.= +rite suspensions in the pres	KOZHAG-0039-0718
rom the volumetric $^3He(n,p)$	^3H reaction.= +deposition in helium f	JAPIAU-0048-3600
coefficient sign reversals in	2H transition metal di chalcogenides.=	PSSBBD-0082-081K
spin members of the 4p-	4h triaxial band in calcium-40.= High-	NUPABL-A285-0253
ute aqueous acid: a corrected	H_A scale.= +de acidity function in dil	CJCHAG-0055-2492
)+ Production of hydrogen(	H_α,H_β) emission in low energy lithium(+	CHPLBC-0049-0346
Production of hydrogen(H_α,	H_β) emission in low energy lithium(+),	CHPLBC-0049-0346
ersonic attenuation near	H_{c1} in superconducting niobium.= Hyp	SSCOA4-0023-0311
f thio+ Applicability of the	H_T acidity function to the protonation o	CJCHAG-0055-2331
o-dimensional Shubnikov-de	Haas conductivity minima.= +is of tw	SSCOA4-0023-0341
dene)-p-butyl aniline) and	HAB (4,4'-di-n-heptyl oxy az oxy benze	MCLCA5-0040-0177
acid contents of normal and	habituated callus.= +ing: free amino	IJEBA6-0015-0581
ntifolia (Christm.) Swing: +	Habituation in root callus of Citrus aura	IJEBA6-0015-0581
llus subtilis by decoyinine or	hadacidin.= +on of sporulation in Baci	BBRCA9-0077-1118
ns in high energy lepton or	hadron scattering off deuteron (nuclei).=	PYLBAJ-069B-0093
=	Hadron shells and spectrum of hadrons.	IVUFAC-20-07-159
deuterium as a probe of	hadron structure.= Double scattering in	PRLTAO-0039-0375
and six quarks.= Weak	hadronic currents in models with four	IDFZA7-0026-0391
photon e^+e^-+ Production of	hadrons and polarization effects in two-	IDFZA7-0026-0384
of	hadrons.= Hadron shells and spectrum	IVUFAC-20-07-159
CVC for gluons and	hadroproduction of quark flavors.=	PYLBAJ-069B-0105
micin against Neisseria and	Haemophilus, including penicillinase-pr	AMACCQ-0012-0293
or pressure of zirconium and	hafnium acetyl acetonate.= +ated vap	VMUKA5-0018-0238

e reaction of zirconium and	hafnium tetra fluorides with calcium flu	VMUKA5-0018-0245
s of titanium, zirconium, and	hafnium.= +sitions in acid phosphate	ZNOKAQ-0022-2065
Crystal structure of the	hafnium-nickel-silicon ($Hf_3Ni_2Si_3$) comp	KRISAJ-0022-0726
an α-feto protein (HAFP);	HAFP monomers and multimers and a r	JOIMA3-0119-0555
by human α-feto protein (	HAFP); HAFP monomers and multimer	JOIMA3-0119-0555
resistance of the root	hair of Trianea bogotensis.= Membrane	FZRSAV-0024-0863
endent methods.=	Half-life of plutonium-239 by two indep	PRVCAN-0016-0354
um chloride+ The F center	half-width in potassium cyanide-potassi	PSSBBD-0082-103K
teraction of rubber with poly	halide compounds.= +oxides on the in	KOZHAG-0039-0816
es in the afterglow of alkali	halide crystals doped with lanthanides.=	OPSPAM-0043-0382

ve reduction of tri- and di-	halogeno methyl compounds to lower ha	CPBTAL-0025-1749
verlap parameters for tetra	halogeno-complexes of copper(II) and co	JCDTBI-1977-1617
a+ Effects of morphine and	haloperidol on the electrical activity of r	JPETAB-0202-0429
duced in monkeys by chronic	haloperidol treatment.= +disorders in	PSCHDL-0053-0289
ine catalepsy.=	Haloperidol-induced tolerance to morph	LIFSAK-0021-0419
kinase from the moderate	halophile, Vibrio costicola.= Pyruvate	CJBIAE-0055-0825
nase isolated from extremely	halophilic bacteria of the Dead Sea. +e	BICHAW-0016-3781
nase isolated from extremely	halophilic bacteria of the Dead Sea. +e	BICHAW-0016-3786
indole in cells of extremely	halophilic bacteria.= Occurrence of	CJMIAZ-0023-0826
Simultaneous separation of	halophilic proteins and nucleic acids a	CJBIAE-0055-0904
ono esters of sucrose and tre	halose.= +c behaviors of fatty acyl m	CPBTAL-0025-1717
osporins to 7α-meth oxy cep	halosporins.= +l conversion of cephal	JACSAT-0099-5504
ynthesis of 7α-meth oxy cep	halosporins.= +. An application to a s	CPBTAL-0025-1645
to 7α-meth oxy cep	halosporins.= A novel synthetic route	JACSAT-0099-5505
7-meth oxy cep	halosporins.= Synthetic studies on	YGKKAE-0035-0563
The action of	halothane on adenylate cyclase.=	MOPMA3-0013-0976
on measures and hydrogen(	$H\alpha$) emission measures: limits on the ele	ASJOAB-0216-0433
od constituents of Rita rita (	Ham.).= +ct of cold shock on some blo	IJEBA6-0015-0568
ituents of cat fish Rita rita (	Ham.).= +rvation on some blood const	IJEBA6-0015-0569
corresponding states.=	Hamaker constants and the principle of	JPCHAX-0081-1631
metals.= Model	Hamiltonian in the theory of transition	IVUMAX-77-07-125
pec+ The application of the	Hammett equation to carbon-13 NMR s	AJCHAS-0030-1715
ers cell s+ Pretreatment of	hamster cells with phen ethyl alcohol alt	CJMIAZ-0023-0835

rved ade⁻ mutant of Chinese	hamster cells.= +over in a purine-sta	JBCHA3-0252-5350
se) polymerase from baby-	hamster kidney cells (BHK-21/C13).=	BCSTB5-0005-0743
1-deoxy cortico sterone by a	hamster liver enzyme.= +de chain of 1	BICHAW-0016-3803
an enzyme preparation from	hamster liver.= +l carboxylic acids by	BICHAW-0016-3810
short-term organ cultures of	hamster lung.= +y benzo(a)pyrene by	BCPCA6-0026-1481
ting on bile salt pool sizes of	hamsters and rats.= +the effects of fas	STEDAM-0029-0695
nthesis in lives of dystrophic	hamsters.= +mounts of hemoglobin sy	CJBIAE-0055-0894
led neutron-activated talc in	hamsters.= +ion and clearance of inha	FCTXAV-0015-0213
rk production through left-	handed currents and lepton number non	PYLBAJ-069B-0065
	Handmade paper of Japan.=	KAGIAU-0031-0590
modif+ Regulation of anti-	hapten antibody response by chemically	IMMUAM-0033-0199
pecificity of interactions of	hapten side chains with the combining s	BIJOAK-0165-0227
prior to immunization with a	hapten-carrier conjugate.= +rophages	IMMUAM-0033-0269
in mice. VIII. A possible +	Hapten-specific IgE antibody responses	JOIMA3-0119-0685
-hexaose derivatives with H-	haptenic structure.= +three lacto-N	ABBIA4-0182-0546
ure of trans-anti-bis(penta	hapto cyclo pentadienyl)di carbonyl bis(	ACBCAR-0B33-2432
and porcine	haptoglobins.= Hybridization of human	IJBOBV-0008-0511
ne of Escherichia coli K-12	harboring a temperature sensitive R pla	BBRCA9-0077-0939
no acid composition of dark	hard and yellow hard kernels separated	CECHAF-0054-0778
atrix selection rules for	hard composite substances.= Particle-m	PHMAA4-0035-1675
Deformation of copper and	hard copper alloys in a rolling mill.=	MTLLAF-0031-0855
l in finite nuclei from Reid's	hard core interaction.= +odel potentia	PRVCAN-0016-0080
ing of helium atoms from a	hard corrugated surface model using the	JCPSA6-0067-0897

ion of dark hard and yellow	hard kernels separated from red winter	CECHAF-0054-0778
r, and wear characteristics of	hard metals.= +, stress intensity facto	AREIAT-0048-0461
gebra model of currents with	hard pions.= +pions on nuclei in the al	IDFZA7-0026-0312
Microwave conditioning of	hard red spring wheat. I. Effects of wide	CECHAF-0054-0717
etrol+ Steels for thermally	hardenable electrically welded gas and p	MTOMAX-77-07-051
properties of a precipitation-	hardened copper alloy.= +ture elastic	ZEMTAE-0068-0506
M5FA ste+ Formation of a	hardened layer during cold rolling of 55S	MTOMAX-77-07-068
copp+ Plotting of curves of	hardening and diagrams of plasticity for	TVMTAX-77-07-060
ed steels with carbo nitride	hardening for gas pipeline tubes with lar	MTOMAX-77-07-041
lt and molybdenum on the	hardening of chromium-nickel stainless	MTOMAX-77-07-002
influence of dopants on the	hardening of gallium arsenide.= The	JAPIAU-0048-3614

halogen bridging in cadmium	halide–poly ether adducts. +tion, and	JCDTBI-1977-1640
e matrix isolation of metal	halide, ligand conformation, and halogen	JCDTBI-1977-1640
change between methylene	halides and ionic halides in water–methy	JCPKBH-1977-1462
methyl compounds to lower	halides by nickel tetra carbonyl.= +no	CPBTAL-0025-1749
w+ Solubilities of the silver	halides in propylene carbonate mixtures	CJCHAG-0055-2499
ethylene halides and ionic	halides in water–methylene halide two–p	JCPKBH-1977-1462
tri alkyl borates with allylic	halides or 2–propynylic halides.= +thyl	BCSJA8-0050-2199
, samarium, and ytterbium	halides to bivalent state in solutions of h	ZNOKAQ-0022-2130
Complexes of boron tri	halides with aromatic azo compounds.=	KOKHDC-0003-1181
toionization of carbon tetra	halides with noble gas resonance radiati	JCPSA6-0067-1091
Condensation of aromatic	halides with olefin in the presence of pa	CHDCAQ-0285-0081
n vacancy motion in alkali	halides with the sodium chloride–type st	PLRBAQ-0016-0947
or tri methyl antimony(V) di	halides.+ Normal coordinate analyses f	JMOSA3-0066-0331
echanics of saturated organic	halides. Part I. Mono ch+ Molecular m	JMOSB4-0040-0127
acement in basic aluminum	halides: $Al_{10}X_4(OH)_{26}(H_2O)_{13}$ and $Al_{10}X$	CHDCAQ-0285-0069
exes initiated by mercury(II)	halides.= +l)di carbonyl iron(II) compl	JACSAT-0099-5295
transition in alkali	halides.= On the polymorphic phase	PSSBBD-0082-0557
silver and thallium	halides.= Photoelastic constants in	SSCOA4-0023-0329
cesium	halides.= Quaternary system of	ZNOKAQ-0022-2227
synthesis of vanadium(II)	halides.= Simple electrochemical	CJCHAG-0055-2631
es of Group IV element tetra	halides.= +trogen–containing complex	KOKHDC-0003-1192
llylic halides or 2–propynylic	halides.= +thyl tri alkyl borates with a	BCSJA8-0050-2199
methane with primary alkyl	halides.= +(di methyl amino)di phenyl	ZECEAL-0017-0259
sition metal di chalcogeni+	Hall coefficient sign reversals in 2H tran	PSSBBD-0082-081K
ition in metal–ammonia so+	Hall effect at the metal–non metal trans	CJCHAG-0055-2240
nide glasses.=	Hall effect in cadmium, germanium arse	PHMAA4-0035-1633
y,+ In situ measurement of	Hall effect, magnetoresistance, resistivit	JAPIAU-0048-3455
reparation and trials of N–	halo acetyl amines as inhibitors of catec	ANQUBU-0072-1018
Co–Co) compound+ [(μ_2–Di	halo acetylene)hexa carbonyl di cobalt](	MGKFA3-0083-0323
elimination of halogen from	halo aklanes by chromous, cuprous, and	CJCHAG-0055-2420
. The+ Rearrangements in	halo alk oxy(thio, amino)–s–tri azines. II	KGSSAQ-1977-0989
route'.=+ Sulfenes from 1–	halo alkane sulfinic acids: the 'abnormal	CJCHAG-0055-2323
o)alkanide anions.= α–	Halo alkyl selenides and α–(phenyl selen	ANCEAD-0089-0561
organic compounds. XVIII.	Halo cyclo pentadienyl iron complexes o	JORCAI-0136-011C
n the carbenoid carbon of α–	halo cyclo propyl lithium. +stitution o	BCSJA8-0050-2158
morphine series, XXI. C–6–	halo derivatives of di hydro codeine.=	MGKFA3-0083-0327
and characterization of penta	halo mono carbonyl osmates(III).= +s	JORCAI-0135-0221
emisorption of simple– and	halo–substituted unsaturated hydro carb	PRLAAZ-0356-0047
mational equilibriums of 8–	halo–8,9,10,11–tetra hydro–7H–cyclo oct	CMLTAG-1977-0897
theses with electrogenerated	halog ens. Part I. Phosphorous ac+ Syn	JESOAN-0124-1175
theses with electrogenerated	halog ens. Part II. Oxidation of m+ Syn	JESOAN-0124-1177
e, ligand conformation, and	halogen bridging in cadmium halide–pol	JCDTBI-1977-1640
ectrosynthesis of organic N–	halogen compounds. (3). Synthesis+ El	DKOKAZ-0045-0475
alides and ionic halides in+	Halogen exchange between methylene h	JCPKBH-1977-1462
the reductive elimination of	halogen from halo aklanes by chromous,	CJCHAG-0055-2420
glet+ Effect of methyl and	halogen substituents on the decay of sin	CHPLBC-0049-0243
f molecular complexes in the	halogen–olefin oxide systems.= +pes o	VMUKA5-0018-0181
d Metabolism and toxicity of	halogenated carb anilides: absorption,	FCTXAV-0015-0205
the torsional angles in 2,6–di	halogenated derivatives.= +igation of	JACSAT-0099-5249
agents.= Limitations of	halogenated hydro carbons as quenching	CHIMAD-0031-0281
Kendall's treatment to the	halogenation of aniline, o–, m–, p–toluid	IJSBDB-015B-0480
4H–1,2–diazepines and their	halogenations.= +hydro–3,7–di aryl–	BCSJA8-0050-2153

funnel for work with	harmful substances.= Separatory	KHSHAY-77-04-085
.= Biosynthesis of a	harmine alkaloid in ethanolic catabolism	ANQUBU-0072-1015
nd–free transitions between	harmonic and flat potentials using exact	JMOSA3-0066-0357
Predissociation of the	harmonic oscillator.=	CHPLBC-0049-0508
ship of excystment agents of	Hartmannella culbertsoni.= +relation	IJEBA6-0015-0542
ificant differences between	Hartree–Fock and local–exchange energy	PRLTAO-0039-0418
ergy bands in po+ Ab initio	Hartree–Fock crystal orbital studies. En	JCPSA6-0067-1180
al Xα exchange and ordinary	Hartree–Fock exchange.= +ted by loc	CHPLBC-0049-0491
ion–interactio+ Generalized	Hartree–Fock natural–orbital configurat	CHPLBC-0049-0555
Adiabatic time–dependent	Hartree–Fock theory in nuclear physics.	NUPABL-A285-0269
ge of McIntosh+ Effects of	harvest date on the condition after stora	CPLSAY-0057-0791
f orchard grass to multiple	harvests and rates of nitrogen in post–se	CPLSAY-0057-0763
partial characterization of	hatching protease of the sea urchin, Stro	ABBIA4-0182-0696
onstituents of Aloe saponaria	Haw. II. The structu+ Studies on the c	CPBTAL-0025-1764
onstituents of Aloe saponaria	Haw. III. The struct+ Studies on the c	CPBTAL-0025-1771
rom Anaphalis morrisonicola	HAY.= +in, an antitumor principle f	JPMSAE-0066-1194
Fire: protection or	hazard by textiles.=	TXLVAE-0012-0320
solutions.= The explosion	hazard of ammoniated silver salt	PSENAC-0021-0221
aration of poly nitr+ A low	hazard procedure for the laboratory prep	SYNTBF-1977-0484
+ I, H + ClBr → HCl + Br,	HBr + Cl.= +cts. X. H + ICl → HCl	CMPHC2-0023-0167
phile, Thermus thermophilus	HB8.= +–1) from an extreme thermo	JOBIAO-0082-0437
ammalian gonadrotropins (	HCG and PMSG) on testicular andro ge	GCENA5-0033-0160
an chorionic gonadotropin (	HCG) on testicular fluid secretion after	CHDDAT-0285-0241
s cycle of the rat+ Ovarian	HCG–binding capacity during the estrou	ACENA7-0085-0850
in or luteinizing hormone (	hCG/LH) receptor and its purification a	ABBIA4-0182-0420
ICl → HCl + I, H + ClBr →	HCl + Br, HBr + Cl.= +cts. X. H +	CMPHC2-0023-0167
on products. X. H + ICl →	HCl + I, H + ClBr → HCl + Br, HBr +	CMPHC2-0023-0167
hloride di hydrate $C_{23}H_{39}N_2$.	$HCl.2H_2O$.= +ireh di amine F hydro c	ACBCAR-0B33-2392
[$FeSO_4$ + CH_2O + NH_2OH.	HCl] + H_2O} system and clarification of	VMUKA5-0018-0242
mate mono hydrate, $NaUO_2$(	$HCOO)_3.H_2O$.= +sodium uranyl tri for	ACBCAR-0B33-2546
al compression and bcc →	hcp phase transition of iron–cobalt alloy	JAPIAU-0048-3374
nic structure of single–crystal	hcp scandium.= +nation of the electro	PLRBAQ-0016-0731
d–cooled energy cables and	HDPE cooling tubes: status and develop	CITEAH-0049-0549
easurements and analyses for	^3He + ^4He at 15.95 MeV (c.m.).= +m	PRVCAN-0016-0018
o the reactions $^6Li(^3He,t^3He)$	^3He and $^6Li(^3He,^3He^3He)^3H$.= +del t	PRVCAN-0016-0042
neutrons.= The $^6Li(n,d)$	^5He and $^7Li(n,d)^6He$ with 56.3 MeV	PRVCAN-0016-0031
ents and analyses for ^3He +	^4He at 15.95 MeV (c.m.).= +measurem	PRVCAN-0016-0018
ectron spectroscopy helium(	He I) of the di thione, bis imine and mo	JMOSB4-0040-0151
$^6Li(n,d)^5He$ and $^7Li(n,d)$	^6He with 56.3 MeV neutrons.= The	PRVCAN-0016-0031
power in the reaction $^3H(p,n)$	^3He.= +of polarization and analyzing	PRVCAN-0016-0107
n excitation in helium ion (	He^+)/carbon di oxide and hydrogen ion	IJMIBY-0024-0429
n helium from the volumetric	$^3He(n,p)^3H$ reaction.= +r deposition i	JAPIAU-0048-3600
i($^3He,t^3He)^3He$ and $^6Li(^3He$,	$^3He^3He)^3H$.= +del to the reactions ^6L	PRVCAN-0016-0042
ns $^6Li(^3He,t^3He)^3He$ and ^6Li(	$^3He,^3He^3He)^3H$.= +del to the reactio	PRVCAN-0016-0042
ynamics of the reaction H_2^+(	$He,H)HeH^+$. Endoergic channels w+ D	CHPLBC-0049-0273
Chlorine–34 via the ^{32}S(	^3He,p) reaction.=	PRVCAN-0016-0055
model to the reactions ^6Li(	$^3He,t^3He)^3He$ and $^6Li(^3He,^3He^3He)^3H$.=	PRVCAN-0016-0042
chain molecules with a polar	head a scaling description.= +ption of	JOPQAG-0038-0983
an continental margin, Cow	Head klippe, western Newfoundland.=	CLCMAB-0025-0163
ssembly of bacteriophage T4	head–related structures. Assembly o+ A	JMOBAK-0114-0061
of the pupil in idiopathic	headache.= Adrenergic supersensitivity	EXPEAM-0033-1082
ly brominated bi phenyls on	health and performance of pregnant Ho	JDSCAE-0060-1294

FIGURE 6-1. Sample of a keyword-from-title index. (From *Chemical Titles*, 1977 (Sept. 19) No. 19:73.) Material reprinted from Chemical titles is copyrighted by the American Chemical Society and is reproduced with permission. No further copying is permitted.

1303 Zajic JE, Guignard H, Gerson DF
Properties and biodegradation of a bioemulsifier from Corynebacterium hydro carbo clastus.= 1303–20

1321 Tassinari T, Macy C
Differential speed two roll mill pretreatment of cellulosic materials for enzymic hydrolysis.= 1321–30

1331 Gutierrez JR, Erickson LE
Hydro carbon uptake in hydro carbon fermentations.= 1331–49

1351 Klibanov AM, Samokhin GP, Martinek K, Berezin IV
A new approach to preparative enzymic synthesis.= 1351–61

1363 Borzani W, Gregori RE, Vairo ML
Some observations on oscillatory changes in the growth rate of Saccharomyces cerevisiae in aerobic continuous undisturbed culture.= 1363–74

1375 Aris R, Humphrey AE
Dynamics of a chemostat in which two organisms compete for a common substrate.= 1375–86

1387 Wengenmayer F, Linder D, Wallenfels K
1,4-α-Glucan phosphorylase from Klebsiella pneumoniae covalently coupled on porous glass.= 1387–403

1405 Venardos D
pH-activity response for immobilized β-glucosidase.= 1405

1407 Miura Y, Miyamoto K
Oxygen transfer within fungal pellets. Reply to comments.= 1407–9

BICHAW Biochemistry, 16, No. 17 (1977)

3727 Stevens CL, Chay TR, Loga S
Rupture of base pairing in double-stranded poly(ribo adenylic acid)·poly(ribo uridylic acid) by form aldehyde: medium chain lengths.= 3727–39

3740 Byrnes JJ, Downey KM, Que BG, Lee MY, Black VL, So AG
Selective inhibition of the 3' to 5' exo nuclease activity associated with DNA polymerases: a mechanism of mutagenesis.= 3740–6

3746 Tack LO, Simpson RT
Characterization of chromatin modified with ethyl acet imidate.= 3746–53

3754 Van NT, Nazar RN, Sitz TO
Comparative studies on the secondary structure of eukaryotic 5.8S ribosomal RNA.= 3754–9

3760 Streefkerk DG, Glaudemans CP
Binding studies on anti-fructo furanan mouse myeloma immuno globulins A47N, A4, U61, and E109.= 3760–5

3765 Novotny J, Franek F, Margolies MN, Haber E
Amino acid sequence of normal (microheterogeneous) porcine immuno globulin λ chains.= 3765–72

Improved pepsin inhibitor derived from activation peptide 1-16 of porcine pepsinogen.= 3846–9

3850 De-Barry J, Fosset M, Lazdunski M
Molecular mechanism of the cardiotoxic action of a poly peptide neuro toxin from sea anemone on cultured embryonic cardiac cells.= 3850–5

3856 Sadowski JA, Schnoes HK, Suttie JW
Vitamin K ep oxidase: properties and relationship to pro thrombin synthesis.= 3856–63

3864 Faller LD, Baroudy BM, Johnson AM, Ewall RX
Magnesium ion requirements for yeast enolase activity.= 3864–9

3870 Rosenberry TL, Neumann E
Interaction of ligands with acetyl cholin esterase. Use of temperature-jump relaxation kinetics in the binding of specific fluorescent ligands.= 3870–8

3879 Shindo H, Cohen JS, Rupley JA
Self-association of hen egg-white lysozyme as studied by nuclear magnetic resonance.= 3879–82

3883 Brown RD, Brewer CF, Koenig SH
Conformation states of concanavalin A: Kinetics of transitions induced by interaction with manganese(2+) and calcium(2+) ions.= 3883–96

3897 Brouwer M, Bonaventura C, Bonaventura J
Oxygen binding by Limulus polyphemus hemo cyanin: allosteric modulation by chloride ions.= 3897–902

3903 Loyter A, Ben-Zaquen R, Marash R, Milner Y
Dephosphorylation of human erythrocyte membranes induced by Sendai virus.= 3903–9

3910 Habener JF, Chang HT, Potts JT
Enzymic processing of proparathyroid hormone by cell-free extracts of parathyroid glands.= 3910–17

3918 Roy AK, Dowbenko DJ
Role of growth hormone in the multihormonal regulation of messenger RNA for α_{2u} globulin in the liver of hypophysectomized rats.= 3918–22

3922 Malchy BL
Studies on the reactive properties of histone amino groups: reactivities of free histones and histones in chromatin as a function of ionic strength.= 3922–7

3928 Pugh CS, Borchardt RT, Stone HO
Inhibition of Newcastle disease virion messenger RNA (guanine-7-)-methyl transferase by analogs of S-adenosyl homo cysteine.= 3928–32

3932 Kremer JM, Van-der-Esker MW, Pathmamanoharan C, Wiersema PH
Vesicles of variable diameter prepared by a modified injection method.= 3932–5

3936 Wu E, Jacobson K, Papahadjopoulos D
Lateral diffusion in phospho lipid multibilayers measured by fluorescence recovery after photobleaching.= 3936–41

BIJOAK Biochem. J., 165, No. 2 (1977)

3777 Letellier L, Weil R, Shechter E
Functional lac carrier proteins in cytoplasmic membrane vesicles isolated from Escherichia coli. 2. Experimental evidence for a segregation of the lac carrier proteins induced by a conformational transition of the membrane lipids.= 3777–80

3781 Mevarech M, Eisenberg H, Neumann E
Malate de hydrogenase isolated from extremely halophilic bacteria of the Dead Sea. 1. Purification and molecular characterization.= 3781–5

3786 Mevarech M, Neumann E
Malate de hydrogenase isolated from extremely halophilic bacteria of the Dead Sea. 2. Effect of salt on the catalytic activity and structure.= 3786–92

3792 Long JW, Dahlquist FW
Evidence for induced interactions in the anticooperative binding of nicotin amide adenine di nucleotide to sturgeon muscle glycer aldehyde–3–phosphate de hydrogenase.= 3792–7

3798 Bigbee WL, Dahlquist FW
Magnetic resonance investigation of ionizable residues at the active site of thermolysin.= 3798–803

3803 Martin KO, Oh SW, Lee HJ, Monder C
Studies on 21–^{3}H–labeled cortico steroids: evidence for isomerization of the ketol side chain of 11–deoxy cortico sterone by a hamster liver enzyme.= 3803–9

3810 Lee HJ, Monder C
Oxidation of cortico steroids to steroidal carboxylic acids by an enzyme preparation from hamster liver.= 3810–14

3815 King HL, Rilling HC
Avian liver prenyl transferase. The role of metal in substrate binding and the orientation of substrates during catalysis.= 3815–19

3820 Matthews RH, Zand R
Basis for substrate preference of amino acid transport system L over amino acid transport system A.= 3820–4

3825 Mecham RP, Foster JA
Trypsin–like neutral protease associated with soluble elastin.= 3825–31

3831 Harkins RN, Black JA, Rittenberg MB
M_2 isozyme of pyruvate kinase from human kidney as the product of a separate gene: its purification and characterization.= 3831–7

3838 Laue MC, Quiocho FA
Spectrochemical and ligand–binding studies of an active mercuri nitro phenol–labeled creatine kinase.= 3838–45

3846 Kumar PM, Kassell B

The gross architecture of an antibody–combining site as determined by spin–label mapping.= 177–97

0199 Willan KJ, Marsh D, Sunderland CS, Sutton BJ, Wain–Hobson S, Dwek RA, Givol D
Comparison of the dimensions of the combining sites of the di nitro phenyl–binding immuno globulin A myeloma proteins MOPC 315, MOPC 460 and XRPC 25 by spin–label mapping.= 199–206

0207 Dower SK, Wain–Hobson S, Gettins P, Givol D, Jackson WR, Perkins SJ, Sunderland CA, Sutton BJ, Wright CE, Dwek RA
The combining site of the di nitro phenyl–binding immuno globulin A myeloma protein MOPC 315.= 207–25

0227 Wain–Hobson S, Dower SK, Gettins P, Givol D, McLaughlin AC, Pecht I, Sunderland CA, Dwek RA
Specificity of interactions of hapten side chains with the combining site of the myeloma protein MOPC 315.= 227–35

0237 Pays E
Characterization of double–stranded ribo nucleic acid sequences present in the initial transcription products of rat liver chromatin.= 237–45

0247 Lindsay JA, Creaser EH
Purification and properties of histidinol de hydrogenases from psychrophilic, mesophilic and thermophilic bacilli.= 247–53

0255 Thorneley RN, Cornish–Bowden A
Kinetics of nitrogenase of Klebsiella pneumoniae. Heterotropic interactions between magnesium–adenosine 5'–di phosphate and magnesium–adenosine 5'–tri phosphate.= 255–62

0263 Corbett MD, Chipko BR
N–Phenyl glycol hydroxamate production by the action of trans ketolase on nitroso benzene.= 263–7

0269 Ogawa N, Thompson T, Friesen HG, Martin JB, Brazeau P
Properties of soluble somatostatin–binding protein.= 269–77

0279 Kiener PA, Waley SG
Substrate–induced deactivation of penicillinases. Studies of β–lactamase I by hydrogen exchange.= 279–85

0287 Hovingh P, Linker A
Specificity of flavobacterial glyc uronidases acting on di saccharides derived from glycos amino glycans.= 287–93

0295 Crowder SE, Ragan CI
Effects of proteolytic digestion by chymotrypsin on the structure and catalytic properties of reduced nicotin amide–adenine di nucleotide–ubi quinone oxido reductase from bovine heart mitochondria.= 295–301

0303 Parr DM
Fragments produced by digestion of human immuno globulin G subclasses with pepsin in urea.= 303–8

FIGURE 6-2. Sample of a list of references included in keyword-from-title index. (From *Chemical Titles*, 1977 (Sept. 19) No. 19:15 B.) Material reprinted from Chemical titles is copyrighted by the American Chemical Society and is reproduced with permission. No further copying is permitted.

the accession number or a unique code for the indexed document is derived by the computer. Then a computer program is used to check each word in a given title against a list of delete words. All title words except words on the delete word list are listed as access points in the index.

Delete words are syntactical in nature and do not carry any message, such as articles, prepositions, and pronouns. Also included in a delete list may be very broad terms that would be of little use as access points in an index. In, for example, a collection of articles on librarianship, the word "librarianship" would be of little value as an access point in an index because it would appear in so many titles. In the example shown in Figure 6-1, note that the access point is given in the center of the page and is surrounded by other title words, hence the term "keyword-in-context."

Figure 6-1 shows an extract from *Chemical Titles*, a keyword-from-title index to chemical journals. The sample page lists entries indexed under the term "hamster," as well as other words. If we look on this page under "hamster liver enzyme," we will note a code on the right-hand side of the line: "BICHAW 0016-3803." This is an example of an abbreviated document code used to refer the reader to fuller bibliographic information in another section. Full bibliographic citations for this entry are given in a separate section of the index, illustrated in Figure 6-2. In Figure 6-2 we see that BICHAW 0016-3803 refers to an article by Martin, K. O., Oh, S. W., Lee, H. J., and Monder, C., "Studies on 21 3H-labeled cortico-steroids: Evidence for isomerization of the ketol side chain of 11-deoxy cortico sterone by a hamster liver enzyme," which appeared in *Biochemistry*, Volume 16, No. 17 (1977), pp. 3803–3809.

Of course, "hamster" is only one of the access points under which this document would be indexed in a keyword-from-title index. Other keywords in the title that could be used as access points include "cortico-steroids," "isomerization," and "ketol." If a searcher were not able to match his search terms with one or more words actually used in the title, however, he would miss this document entirely. If, for instance, the searcher looked under the term "rodent" rather than "hamster," this document would not be picked up because the term "rodent" does not appear in the document title.

A keyword-from-title index is typically based only on words appearing in document titles and *does not* include "see" or "see also" cross-references, providing no assistance in suggesting access points to search. It is thus an index in which no attempt is made to provide vocabulary control, and for this reason is difficult to search. To identify all possible index terms, the searcher must consider all the possible ways in which a topic might have been described in a document title. Later in this chapter we show how to use vocabulary aids prepared for other indexes to suggest additional index terms for searching a keyword-from-title index.

Citation Indexes

Another type of index you are likely to encounter in reference work is the citation index, an example of which is given in Figure 6-3. To understand citation indexes, you must first understand the terms "cited reference" and "citing reference." A cited reference is a document referred to in a publication, listed either as a footnote or in the bibliography. A citing reference is the publication in which this footnote or bibliography appears. As an example, we might search the index extract in Figure 6-3 (from the *Social Science Citation Index*) for a 1968 article by K. Wright, entitled "Driver Eye Fixation," which is listed as a cited reference. Under the cited reference, "Wright," we find the citing reference: an article by D. Shinar published in the journal, *Human Factors*, Volume 19, 1977. If we then look under the citing reference, "Shinar," we find the following: "Shinar, D., McDowell, Ed., and Rockwell, Th., "Eye-movements in Curve Negotiation," *Human Factors* 19 (1): 63–71 (1977)." In this example, then, Wright is the cited reference and Shinar is the citing reference.

The conventional way in which we identify citations is in a list of cited references appearing in a citing reference (or document). The citation index reverses this arrangement by using the cited reference as an access point, and listing one or more citing references under this cited reference. Thus, the arrangement is by cited reference, with all citing references listed below the cited reference. In the illustrated example, only an abbreviated citation is given for each item. Fuller citations are given in another volume of this index, the listing of citing references—in this case, Shinar, McDowell, and Rockwell. This is called the "source index," and an extract of it is included as Figure 6-4.

USING A CITATION INDEX

How are citation indexes used by reference librarians? One of the uses of such indexes is to verify bibliographic citations. When an incomplete citation needs to be identified, the *Science Citation Index* and the *Social Science Citation Index* are useful tools because they systematically index citations appearing in the important journals in the natural sciences and social sciences. This is particularly helpful when you do not know the specific discipline within these sciences to which a reference pertains.

A second use of citation indexes is for subject searches. This may appear strange because citation indexes do not provide the conventional subject approach that we have previously discussed. However, by citing a document, an author indicates a relationship between the topic about which he is writing

WRIGHT JV			VOL	PG	YR
RAMSDEN PG	AM ANTIQUIT	B	42	146	77
WRIGHT JW					
52 46 US FOR SERV NE FO					
OGDEN JG	ANN NY ACAD	R	288	16	77
WRIGHT K					
68 DRIVER EYE FIXATION					
SHINAR D	HUMAN FACT		19	63	77
WRIGHT KC					
72 TRENDS MODERN SUBJEC					
MACGREGO J	J HIGH EDUC		48	17	77
WRIGHT L					
" DISPLAY DUTIE 37					
BERNSTELDM	PSYCHIAT AN		7	92	77
47 ATLANTIC FRONTIER 8					
SWIERENG RP	SOCIAL SCIE		52	31	77
67 AM PSYCHOLOGIST 22 323					
DROTAR D	PROF PSYCHO		8	72	77
73 CLIN PEDIAT 12 594					
REINHART JB	PEDIATRICS		59	371	77
74 J CLIN CHILD PSYCHOL 3 37					
PEARSE M	J SCH HEALT		47	174	77
74 J CLINICAL CHILD PSY 4 13					
76 CLINICAL PSYCHOLOGIS 29 16					
DROTAR D	PROF PSYCHO		8	72	77
WRIGHT LB					
40 COMMUNICATION 93					
40 1ST GENTLEMEN VIRGIN 57					
BREEN TH	WILLIAM M Q		34	239	77
40 1ST GENTLEMEN VIRGIN 261					
CHARPENT AA	LAW LIBR J	D	69	576	76
41 SECRET DIARY W BYRD 223					
BREEN TH	WILLIAM M Q		34	239	77
53 COLONIAL SEARCH SOUT 44					
65 DREAM PROSPERITY COL					
65 ELIZABETHANS AM COLL 253					
66 PROSE WORKS W BYRD W 19					

FIGURE 6-3. Sample of a citation index. (From *Social Science Citation Index* (January–April 1977):column 4968.)

PASAMANICK B	60	AM J PUBL HLTH	50	1737
"	66	MERRILL PALMER QUART	12	7
RUTSTEIN DO	52	AM J DISEASES CHILDR	84	199
TORREY EF		IN PRESS		
"	73	LANCET	2	22
"	73	SCHIZOPHREMIA B	7	53
"	74	LANCET	2	942
"	76	SCHIZ B	12	236
TORREY RF	74	AM J PSYCHIATRY	131	567
TRAMER M	29	SCHWELZ ARCH MEUROL	24	17
VIDEBECH T	74	ACTA PSYCHIAT SCAND	50	202
WOODRUFF RA	74	AM J PSYCHIATRY	131	925

SHIN HK

see BELL RR J NUTR 107 42 77

SHINAR D

MCDOWELLED ROCKWELLTH—EYE-MOVEMENTS IN CURVE NEGOTIATION

HUMAN FACT *19(1):63–71* *77* *15R*

INDIANA UNIV. BLOOMINGTON, IN 47401, USA

BHISE VC	71	1971 P ANN M AM ASS		
FRY GA	68	AM J OPTOMETRY ARCH	45	374
GORDON DA	66	PUBLIC ROADS	34	53
HARTMANN E	70	1970 INT AUT SAF C N		
HERRIN GD			16	129
KAHNEMAN D	70	ACIA PSYCHOLOGICA	33	118
MACKWORTH NH	67	PERCEPTION PSYCHOPHY	2	547
MOURANT RR	72	HUMAN FACTORS	14	325
ROCKWELL TH	72	HUMAN FACTORS HIGHWA		
"	72	6TH P C AUSTR ROAD R	6	316
SAFFORD RR	71	THESIS OHIO STATE U		
SHINAR D	75	54TH TRANSP RES BOAR		
WRIGHT K	68	DRIVER EYE FIXATION		
VARBUS AL	67	EYE MOVEMENTS VISION		
ZUSNE L	64	PERCEPTUAL MOTOR SKI	18	11

SHINDO H

■ MIYAKOSH N—WHOLE-BODY AUTORADIOGRAPHIC STUDIES ON DISTRIBUTION OF C-14-LABELED D-5-HYDROXYTRYPTOPHAN AND L-5-HYDROXYTRYPTOPHAN, 5-HYDROXYTRYPTAMINE AND 5-HYDROXYINDOLE-3-ACETIC ACIDS IN RATS

CHEM PHARM *24(12):3158–3168* *76* *14R*

SANKYO CO LTD. CENT RES LABS. SHINAGAWA KU, TOKYO JAPAN

(ANON)	74	94TH ANN M PHARM SOC		
COPPEN A	72	J PSYCHIAT RES	9	163
COTZIAS GC	69	NEW ENGL J MED	280	337
KASHIMA M	67	NIPPON ACTA RADIOLOG	27	315
LAPIN IP	69	LANCET	1	132
MIYAKOSHI N		TO BE PUBLISHED		
RITZEN M	65	BIOCHEM PHARMACOL	14	313
SANO I	72	FOLIA PSYCHIAT NEURO	26	7
SHINDO H		IN PRESS		
"	71	CHEM PHARM	19	2490
"	72	"	20	966
"	73	CHEM PHARM B TOKYO	21	826
TAKAHASHI S	75	J PSYCHIAT RES	11	1
VANPRAAG HM	72	PSYCHOPHARMACOLOGIA	25	14

FIGURE 6-4. Sample of a source index for a citation index. [From *Social Science Citation* Index, "Source Index" (January–April, 1977): column 2942.]

(the citing reference) and each document he cites (the cited references). This relationship may be one of general background on a subject, may refer to earlier work in the field, or to a technique used, just to give some examples. By searching under each cited reference, you can locate other documents by authors who utilized and cited this reference since its publication. By looking up cited references listed under a citing reference, you may obtain more recent information on the subject. It is thus a way of bringing work forward in time. However, you must have a specific citation, the cited reference, to access the index.

Coordinate Indexes

The last type of index we shall discuss is the coordinate index. This is the type of index used in machine-readable bibliographic files such as the on-line searched indexes to be covered in Chapter 10. As with all other types of indexes except the citation index, the basic unit of the coordinate index is the index entry, which consists of the index heading and document identification. In a coordinate index, this index heading is called a "descriptor."

There is a main difference between coordinate indexes and other types of indexes, excluding citation indexes. For most types of indexes, the indexer (human or computer) selects the terms (words or phrases) under which the document will be indexed. Thus the index heading (descriptor) and associated document accession number or other document identification become the index entry. With coordinate indexes also, the indexer, which again may be human or computer, selects the index headings (descriptors) under which the document will be indexed, and adds the document identification. Up to this point, the procedure is identical for all the previously discussed indexes (except the citation index). However, the coordinate index differs in the flexibility it offers for searching index headings. While other indexes must be searched by using single index headings (selected by the indexer at the time of indexing), the coordinate index can also be searched by using *combinations of descriptors selected at the time of searching the index.*

The descriptors are building blocks that may be searched singly or combined (coordinated) with any other descriptors to form a desired search heading. The possibility of combining or coordinating descriptors to form more specific or more generic search headings creates the flexibility of this index. The indexer does not have to decide at the time of indexing a document what combinations of terms to include in an index because with a coordinate index any descriptor can, at least in theory, be combined with any other descriptor by the searcher. Most computer-searched indexes are coordinate indexes because of the capabilities of the computer to search and exploit the flexibility of this type of index.

The ways in which individual descriptors can be combined or coordinated at the time of searching a coordinate index will now be illustrated. As an example, we use the following sample descriptors from an index vocabulary of a hypothetical coordinate index. Each of these descriptors is also assigned a letter as a shorthand notation.

Academic Libraries	(A)	Cost	(I)
Public Libraries	(B)	Accuracy	(J)
School Libraries	(C)	Speed	(K)
Special Libraries	(D)	1960–1965	(L)
Acquisition	(E)	1966–1970	(M)
Cataloging	(F)	1971–1975	(N)
Circulation	(G)	1976–date	(O)
Reference	(H)		

Each of these 15 descriptors (labeled with the shorthand notations A–O) can be searched singly, as, for example, in a search for all documents dealing with Academic Libraries (A). The coordinate index can also be searched using any combination of these descriptors. Possible combinations of descriptors are characterized into three main types, called logical products, logical sums, and logical differences.

Following are examples of the different types of searches, with an explanation of what happens when descriptors are so combined.

Logical Product: *A and H and J (Academic Libraries* and *Reference and Accuracy)*. Note that the connector-operator *and* is used between descriptors. This specifies that all descriptors in the search statement must be present in order to select a document. There is no theoretical limitation as to the number of descriptors that can be included in a logical product statement. It stands to reason that, beyond a certain number of descriptors specified in the search statement, no document will be retrieved because no document is likely to satisfy, say, each of 10 specified descriptors.

Logical Sum: *A or B or C or D (Academic Libraries or Public Libraries or School Libraries or Special Libraries)*. This type of search statement calls for documents indexed under at least one of the four descriptors, either A *or* B *or* C *or* D. The logical connector-operator in this case is the *or*, and this type of search statement is used to search for a more generic term by listing all possible specific terms under which a broad subject may be indexed. In the example, the search is for the generic term "libraries," made up by requesting documents on any of four specific types of libraries.

Logical Difference: *C and not L* (*School Libraries and not 1960–1965*). What is being called for here is a collection of articles on school libraries that were published after 1965. The connector in this case is *and not*. It specifies the presence of one descriptor (the one to the left of the *and not* connector, in this case, C) and the absence of another descriptor (the one to the right of the *and not* connector, L).

The logical-difference search connector is used primarily for groups of descriptors that are mutually exclusive, i.e., only one descriptor from that group has been selected for indexing any one document. The date of the document is an example of such a mutually exclusive descriptor category. When descriptors from a non-mutually exclusive category are used with the *and not* connector, the searcher may exclude potentially relevant documents. If we search for articles on Academic Libraries and not Public Libraries (A and not B), articles dealing simultaneously with both Academic *and* Public Libraries will be rejected, even though they might be relevant, because the *and not* connector is given preference in executing the search statement. Thus care must be taken in using the *and not* search logic to insure that potentially relevant documents are not rejected.

In addition, searches can be made using combinations of two or all three of these types of searches. For example, a single search statement could be constructed using either logical product and logical sum, logical product and logical difference, or logical sum and logical difference.

Logical Product and Logical Sum: *(A or B or C) and H*. This is a commonly used type of search statement specifying the presence of any one of several descriptors (A or B or C) in combination with H. The grouping in parentheses is the logical sum part of the search statement, while the *and* operator makes this a logical product search as well. For this search, documents with the following descriptors would be selected: A and H; B and H; and C and H (which would deal with reference in Academic or Public or School Libraries). Documents with A and B and H (Academic Libraries, Public Libraries, Reference), or A and B and C and H (Academic Libraries, Public Libraries, School Libraries, Reference) would also be selected because they meet the minimum specifications of one descriptor from the (A or B or C) group.

Logical Product and Logical Difference: A logical product and difference search would be: A and B, not C (Academic and Public Libraries, not School Libraries).

Logical Sum and Logical Difference: *(A or B or C) and not D*. Here we are asking for documents on Academic or Public or School Libraries but not Special Libraries. Search statements with logical difference, the *and not* operator, are always potentially troublesome because they have a tendency to reject not only nonrelevant but also relevant documents, as we have already mentioned.

With these few types of search statements, any complex search may be formulated. This makes the coordinate index an index with considerable flexibility. More will be said about it in Chapter 10 when we discuss on-line searched bibliographic data bases.

INDEX VOCABULARY AIDS

It is likely that the message words used in a patron's query statement will not be the same words or phrases used as the headings in an index. A bridging tool needs to be used to bring the vocabulary used in the query to coincide with the vocabulary of the index.

Some indexes include vocabulary aids to assist index users. *See* and *see also* are vocabulary aids interfiled with the index entries to direct the searcher to the terms selected as index headings and to related index headings for locating additional and potentially relevant documents. There may also be separate listings of terms that may aid in identifying potentially useful index headings. These listings are called subject authority lists and thesauri. The two terms are often used interchangeably, although they are not identical. The subject authority list suggests synonyms and otherwise related terms to search. The thesaurus performs this function but also lists more specific as well as more generic index terms.

Subject Authority List

The subject authority list is designed as the master list of terms used in the index as an aid to both the indexer and the searcher. It consists of alphabetically arranged subject headings along with "see," "see also," "see from," and "see also from" references, and also "scope notes" (brief explanations of the scope or meaning of terms). An example of a subject authority list used in cataloging is the Library of Congress List of Subject Headings, a most useful tool for locating subject headings in the card catalog (as we described in Chapter 5).

Thesaurus

A thesaurus provides, in addition to an alphabetic list of index headings and cross-references, a hierarchical list of the terms used in the index. Under individual descriptors, the thesaurus also lists more specific and more generic index terms. A sample page excerpt from a thesaurus, the *Thesaurus of ERIC Descriptors* (6th ed., 1975, p. 143), is given in Figure 6-5.

Social History
Sociocultural Patterns

LIFTING Jul. 1966
SN Act of raising or elevating a weighted object
BT Physical Activities
RT Exercise (Physiology)
Job Skills
Task Performance

LIGHT Sep. 1968
UF Light Radiation
Optical Spectrum
Visible Radiation
Visible Spectrum
NT Daylight
BT Radiation
RT Climatic Factors
Color
Contrast
Controlled Enviornment
Electrooptics
Environment
Environmental Influences
Glare
Illumination Levels
Lasers
Lighting
Lights
Luminescence
Optics
Photosynthesis
Physics
Relativity

Light Amplifiers (Lasers)
USE LASERS

LIGHTED PLAYGROUNDS Jul. 1966
BT Playgrounds

LIGHTING Jul. 1966
UF Illumination
NT Outdoor Lighting
Television Lighting
RT Building Design
Climate Control
Contrast
Design Needs
Electrical Systems
Flexible Lighting Design
Glare
Heating
Human Engineering
Illumination Levels
Interior Design
Light
Lighting Design
Lights
Luminescence
Optics
Solar Radiation
Utilities
Ventilation
Windowless Rooms
Windows

LIGHTING DESIGN Apr. 1970
NT Flexible Lighting Design
BT Design
RT Architecture
Building Design
Contrast
Design Needs
Glare
Illumination Levels
Interior Design
Lighting
Lights
Outdoor Lighting
Windowless Rooms

Light Radiation
USE LIGHT

LIGHTS Jul. 1966
NT Television Lights
BT Equipment
RT Flexible Lighting Design
Glare
Illumination Levels
Light
Lighting
Lighting Design
Luminescence
Outdoor Lighting

LIMITED EXPERIENCE Jul. 1966
BT Experience
RT Cultural Disadvantagement
Disadvantaged Environment

LINEAR PROGRAMMING Jul. 1966
BT Mathematical Applications
RT Branching
Computers
Mathematical Models
Matrices
Operations Research

LINGALA Jul. 1966
UF Mangala
BT African Languages
Bantu Languages

LINGUISTIC COMPETENCE Mar. 1969
BT Language Skills
RT Cognitive Processes
Comprehension
Linguistic Performance
Linguistics

Linguistic Difficulty (Contrastive)
USE INTEREFERENCE (LANGUAGE LEARNING)

LINGUISTIC DIFFICULTY (INHERENT) Sep. 1974
SN Universal difficulty (or ease) in articulating, auditing, or processing particular linguistic units and unit sequences
RT Language Development
Language Learning Levels
Language Universals
Linguistics
Linguistic Theory
Native Speakers

LINGUISTIC PATTERNS Jul. 1966
RT Language Patterns
Linguistics

LINGUISTIC PERFORMANCE Mar. 1969
BT Performance
Linguistics
Oral Communication
Oral Expression
Speech

LINGUISTICS Jul. 1966
UF Philology
NT Applied Linguistics
Computational Linguistics
Diachronic Linguistics
Distinctive Features
Graphemes
Mathematical Linguistics
Neurolinguistics
Paralinguistics
Psycholinguistics
Sociolinguistics
Structural Linguistics
Synchronic Linguistics
RT American English
Deep Structure
Definitions
Dialects
English
English (Second Language)
Glottochronology
Information Theory
Intonation
Language
Language Ability
Language Research
Language Usage
Linguistic Competence
Linguistic Difficulty (Inherent)
Linguistic Performance
Middle English
Miscue Analysis
Old English
Onomastics
Phoneme Grapheme Correspondence
Phonemics
Semiotics
Sentence Diagraming
Social Dialects
Speech
Speech Education
Structural Analysis
Surface Structure
Traditional Grammar

LINGUISTIC THEORY Jul. 1966
NT Case (Grammar)
Generative Grammar
Generative Phonology
Semiotics
Structural Grammar
Traditional Grammar
RT Componential Analysis
Computational Linguistics
Descriptive Linguistics
Language Universals
Linguistic Difficulty (Inherent)
Neurolinguistics
Nucleation (Language Learning)
Psycholinguistics
Sociolinguistics

Linguistic Universals
USE LANGUAGE UNIVERSALS

LIPREADING Jul. 1966
UF Speech Reading
BT Reading
RT Cued Speech
Deaf Education
Deaf interpreting
Hearing Therapists
Hearing Therapy
Speech Education

FIGURE 6-5. Sample of a thesaurus (alphabetical arrangement). (From *Thesaurus of ERIC Descriptors*, 6th ed., 1975, p. 143)

The thesaurus consists of descriptors selected for indexing and searching the document collection, along with terms leading to these descriptors. The different types of relationships among descriptors and terms not used as descriptors are:

1. *Synonym relationship* (from terms *not used* to the term *selected* as descriptor). *Example*: Light Radiation—use LIGHT. (This is the equivalent to a "see" reference in a card catalog.)
2. *Synonym relationship* (from term *used* as descriptor to term *not used* as descriptor). This is the reciprocal to relationship (1) and is the equivalent to the "see from" reference in the card catalog. *Example*: LIGHT, UF Light Radiation (UF is the abbreviation for "used for").

These descriptors and synonyms are arranged alphabetically in the first part of the thesaurus. In the second part, descriptors without broader descriptors (broader terms, or BTs) are listed alphabetically. Whenever narrower descriptors (narrower terms, or NTs) are included with the listed descriptors, they are given in a hierarchical arrangement from the most generic to the most specific, with each level being indented. This arrangement is illustrated as Figure 6-6.

Although subject authority lists and thesauri are probably the most useful index vocabulary aids, there are other aids that should be consulted. For example, the patron could be asked to suggest additional terms that might be used as subject headings. In regard to this, one other point should be made: Although subject authority lists and thesauri are initially designed to be used with specific indexes, the *New York Times Thesaurus* being designed for the *New York Times Index*, for instance, they may also be useful for suggesting terms to search in other indexes. This type of aid is particularly useful when you are searching indexes without vocabulary control, such as keyword-from-title indexes. In these cases, when the searcher needs to make a list of possible search headings, any subject authority list or thesaurus in the same or a related subject may be useful.)

Keep in mind that there may be errors in the query statement that result in searching difficulties. Some of the more commonly occurring problems include errors in the author's name, in dates, and in spelling or use of words. Authors' names are usually easier to search than subjects because they are less ambiguous access points, but this may only be so if the name of the author has been given correctly. An author's name may also have alternate spellings, for example, Smith and Smyth, and you should consider such possible alternate spellings when searching. Sometimes the components of an author's name may be given in incorrect order. For example, John Paul Irving may turn out to be Irving Paul John or John Irving Paul. To avoid this problem,

..ADULT VOCATIONAL EDUCATION
...ADULT FARMER EDUCATION
..LABOR EDUCATION
..MIGRANT ADULT EDUCATION
..PARENT EDUCATION
..PUBLIC SCHOOL ADULT EDUCATION
..VETERANS EDUCATION
.AEROSPACE EDUCATION
.AESTHETIC EDUCATION
..ART APPRECIATION
..FILM STUDY
..MUSIC APPRECIATION
.AFTER SCHOOL EDUCATION
.ALCOHOL EDUCATION
.ART EDUCATION
.BILINGUAL EDUCATION
.CAREER EDUCATION
.COEDUCATION
.COMMUNITY EDUCATION
.COMPARATIVE EDUCATION
.COMPENSATORY EDUCATION
.COMPUTER SCIENCE EDUCATION
.CONSUMER EDUCATION
..CONSUMER SCIENCE
.CONTINUATION EDUCATION
.CORRECTIONAL EDUCATION
.CORRESPONDENCE STUDY
.CULTURAL EDUCATION
.DRIVER EDUCATION
.DRUG EDUCATION
.EARLY CHILDHOOD EDUCATION
..PRESCHOOL EDUCATION
..PRIMARY EDUCATION
.ECONOMIC EDUCATION
.ELEMENTARY SECONDARY EDUCATION
..ELEMENTARY EDUCATION
...ADULT BASIC EDUCATION
...PRIMARY EDUCATION
..SECONDARY EDUCATION
...COLLEGE PREPARATION
.ENGLISH EDUCATION
.ENVIRONMENTAL EDUCATION
..CONSERVATION EDUCATION
.EQUAL EDUCATION
.EXTENSION EDUCATION
..LIBRARY EXTENSION
..RURAL EXTENSION
..UNIVERSITY EXTENSION
..URBAN EXTENSION
.FAMILY LIFE EDUCATION
..HOMEMAKING EDUCATION
..PARENTHOOD EDUCATION
..SEX EDUCATION
.GENERAL EDUCATION
.HEALTH EDUCATION
.HUMANISTIC EDUCATION
.INDUSTRIAL EDUCATION
.INTERGROUP EDUCATION
.INTERNATIONAL EDUCATION
.LIBRARY EDUCATION
.LITERACY EDUCATION
.MIGRANT EDUCATION
..MIGRANT ADULT EDUCATION
..MIGRANT CHILD EDUCATION
.MUSIC EDUCATION
.NEGRO EDUCATION
.NONDISCRIMINATORY EDUCATION
.NONFORMAL EDUCATION
.OPEN EDUCATION
..EXTERNAL DEGREE PROGRAMS
..SELF DIRECTED CLASSROOMS
.OUTDOOR EDUCATION
.PERFORMANCE BASED EDUCATION
..PERFORMANCE BASED TEACHER EDUCATION
.PHYSICAL EDUCATION
..ADAPTED PHYSICAL EDUCATION
.POPULATION EDUCATION
.POST SECONDARY EDUCATION
..HIGHER EDUCATION
...ALUMNI EDUCATION
...GRADUATE STUDY
...MANAGEMENT EDUCATION
...POST DOCTORIAL EDUCATION
...PROFESSIONAL EDUCATION
....ADMINISTRATOR EDUCATION
....ARCHITECTURAL EDUCATION
....ENGINEERING EDUCATION
....HOME ECONOMICS EDUCATION
....INSERVICE EDUCATION
....MEDICAL EDUCATION
....PROFESSIONAL CONTINUING EDUCATION
....TEACHER EDUCATION
.....INSERVICE TEACHER EDUCATION
.....PERFORMANCE BASED TEACHER EDUCATION
.....PRESERVICE EDUCATION
.....STUDENT TEACHING
......EPISODE TEACHING
.....TEACHER EDUCATOR EDUCATION
....THEOLOGICAL EDUCATION
...PUBLIC ADMINISTRATION EDUCATION
...TERMINAL EDUCATION
...UNDERGRADUATE STUDY
.PROCESS EDUCATION
.PROGRESSIVE EDUCATION
.PUBLIC AFFAIRS EDUCATION
.PUBLIC EDUCATION
..PUBLIC SCHOOL ADULT EDUCATION
.RELIGIOUS EDUCATION
.RURAL EDUCATION
.SAFETY EDUCATION
.SCIENCE EDUCATION
..FLUID POWER EDUCATION
..MATHEMATICS EDUCATION
.SERVICE EDUCATION
.SPECIAL EDUCATION
..ADAPTED PHYSICAL EDUCATION
..DEAF EDUCATION
..EXCEPTIONAL CHILD EDUCATION
..SPEECH EDUCATION
.STUDY ABROAD
.SUPPLEMENTARY EDUCATION
.UNIVERSAL EDUCATION
.URBAN EDUCATION
.VOCATIONAL EDUCATION
..ADULT VOCATIONAL EDUCATION
...ADULT FARMER EDUCATION
..AGRICULTURAL EDUCATION
...ADULT FARMER EDUCATION
...YOUNG FARMER EDUCATION
..BUSINESS EDUCATION
...OFFICE OCCUPATIONS EDUCATION
..COOPERATIVE EDUCATION
..DISTRIBUTIVE EDUCATION
...SALESMANSHIP
..HEALTH OCCUPATIONS EDUCATION
..OCCUPATIONAL HOME ECONOMICS
..PREVOCATIONAL EDUCATION
..TECHNICAL EDUCATION
...FIRE SCIENCE EDUCATION
..TRADE AND INDUSTRIAL EDUCATION
.WOMENS EDUCATION

EDUCATIONAL ALTERNATIVES

EDUCATIONAL BENEFITS

EDUCATIONAL DEMAND

EDUCATIONAL EQUALITY

EDUCATIONAL PRACTICE

EDUCATIONAL QUALITY
TEACHING QUALITY

EDUCATIONAL TRENDS

EFFICIENCY

EIDETIC IMAGES

ELECTRICAL SYSTEMS

ELECTRICITY

ELECTRONIC CLASSROOM USE

ELECTRONIC CONTROL

EMPLOYMENT
.JOBS
..PART TIME JOBS
.MIGRANT EMPLOYMENT
.MULTIPLE EMPLOYMENT
.NEGRO EMPLOYMENT
.OVERSEAS EMPLOYMENT
.SEASONAL EMPLOYMENT
.STUDENT EMPLOYMENT
.SUBEMPLOYMENT
.TEACHER EMPLOYMENT
.YOUTH EMPLOYMENT

EMPLOYMENT LEVEL

EMPLOYMENT PATTERNS

EMPLOYMENT POTENTIAL

EMPLOYMENT PRACTICES

EMPLOYMENT TRENDS

ENERGY
.HEAT
.RADIATION
..LIGHT
..DAYLIGHT
..SOLAR RADIATION

ENGLISH NEOCLASSIC LITERARY PERIOD

ENRICHMENT
.ACADEMIC ENRICHMENT
.CULTURAL ENRICHMENT
.CURRICULUM ENRICHMENT
.LANGUAGE ENRICHMENT
.MATHEMATICAL ENRICHMENT

ENROLLMENT
.AVERAGE DAILY ENROLLMENT
.LANGUAGE ENROLLMENT
.LATE SCHOOL ENTRANCE
.SCHOOL REGISTRATION
.STUDENT ENROLLMENT
..DUAL ENROLLMENT

ENROLLMENT INFLUENCES

ENROLLMENT TRENDS

ENVIROMENT
.CONTROLLED ENVIRONMENT
.CONTROL ENVIRONMENT
.CULTURAL CONTEXT
.CULTURAL ENVIRONMENT
..CULTURAL ISOLATION
.DISADVANTAGED ENVIRONMENT
..CULTURAL DISADVANTAGEMENT
..ECONOMIC DISADVANTAGEMENT
..EDUCATIONAL DISADVANTAGEMENT
..SOCIAL DISADVANTAGEMENT
...SOCIAL ISOLATION
.EDUCATIONAL ENVIRONMENT
..CLASSROOM ENVIRONMENT
..SCHOOL ENVIRONMENT
...COLLEGE ENVIRONMENT
...SCHOOL CONDITIONS
..TEACHING CONDITIONS
.FAMILY ENVIRONMENT
.INSTITUTIONAL ENVIRONMENT
..SCHOOL ENVIRONMENT
...COLLEGE ENVIRONMENT
...SCHOOL CONDITIONS
.PERMISSIVE ENVIRONMENT
.PHYSICAL ENVIRONMENT
..ACOUSTICAL ENVIRONMENT
..CLIMATIC FACTORS
..THERMAL ENVIRONMENT
..VISUAL ENVIRONMENT
.RURAL ENVIRONMENT
.SIMULATED ENVIRONMENT
.SLUM ENVIRONMENT
..SLUM CONDITIONS
.SOCIAL ENVIRONMENT
.SOCIAL ISOLATION
.SUBURBAN ENVIRONMENT
.THERAPEUTIC ENVIRONMENT
.URBAN ENVIRONMENT
..INNER CITY
.WORK ENVIRONMENT

ENVIRONMENTAL INFLUENCES

EQUIPMENT
.ACOUSTIC INSULATION

FIGURE 6-6. Hierarchical display (*Thesaurus of ERIC Descriptors*, 6th ed., 1975, p. 362.)

consider every component of an author's name as a possible family name that could be used as an access point. Dates are also often given inaccurately. A year given by the requestor as 1960 may actually be earlier or later. Differences in spelling and word use between American and British English must also be considered, as for example gasoline and petrol, or sulfur and sulphur. Finally, some indexes use common names of plants and animals and others use the scientific names, usually the Latin names. Here handbooks or dictionaries must be used to make the translation.

SUMMARY

In this chapter three different types of indexes, in addition to the alphabetic subject index, have been briefly described. These are the keyword-from-title index, the citation index, and the coordinate index. Each of these indexes consists of individual index entries made up of the index heading and a document identification. Some of these indexes have elements of vocabulary control to assist the searcher in selecting useful index headings. Subject authority lists and thesauri are examples of vocabulary aids that help bring the vocabulary of the query to coincide with the vocabulary of the index. In Chapter 10, the use of an on-line searched coordinate index with a thesaurus will be illustrated.

QUESTIONS FOR DISCUSSION

If there is a choice between types of access points to use in searching an index, for instance, author *versus* subject, which type of access point would you use and why?

In making a list of index headings to use in searching, what types of terms in addition to those supplied by the patron could you collect?

Why are indexes without vocabulary control considered more difficult to search than indexes with elements of vocabulary control?

EXERCISE 1 Selection of Subject Headings

(For each query, list all potentially relevant subject headings in the indicated volume of *Library Literature*. To complete this exercise, potentially relevant subject headings should be obtained by following "see also" cross-references.)

SAMPLE QUERY: *List subject headings used in the* ***Library Literature*** *1974–1975 volume relating to interlibrary loans.*

ANSWER TO SAMPLE QUERY:

Automation of Library Processes—Interlibrary Loans
College and University Libraries—Interlibrary loans
Industrial Libraries—Interlibrary Loans
Interlibrary Loans
Medical Libraries—Interlibrary Loans
National Libraries—Interlibrary Loans
Public Libraries—Interlibrary Loans
Research Libraries—Interlibrary Loans
Teletype

Queries

1. List search headings in the *Library Literature* 1974–1975 volume dealing with reference books.
2. List subject headings in the *Library Literature* 1974–1975 volume on all aspects of public relations in libraries.

Answers to Exercise 1 are on p. 82.

EXERCISE 2 Search Statement Formulation

(Alphabetically and hierarchically arranged excerpts from a hypothetical subject authority list follow. In these lists, BT = broader term, NT = narrower term, RT = related term, and UF = use for. Assume that you will be searching a coordinate index in which indexing is on a single, most specific level. For example, the concept, "public libraries" would be indexed by the descriptor Public Libraries only. For the preparation of search statements, assume that you are attempting to locate all potentially relevant documents on a subject.)

Extract of Subject Authority List (Alphabetic Arrangement)

Academic Libraries
  BT Libraries
  NT College Libraries
  NT Junior College Libraries
  NT University Libraries
Accuracy
  BT Evaluation
Clerks
  BT Staffing

College Libraries
BT Academic Libraries
Community College Libraries
Use
Junior College Libraries
Cost
BT Evaluation
Evaluation
NT Accuracy
NT Cost
NT Timeliness
RT Standards
Information Services
NT Interlibrary Loans
NT Literature Searching
NT Reference Service
NT Referral Service
Interlibrary Loans
BT Information Services
Junior College Libraries
BT Academic Libraries
UF Community College Libraries
Librarians
BT Staffing
Libraries
NT Academic Libraries
NT Public Libraries
NT School Libraries
NT Special Libraries
Literature Searching
BT Information Services
Media Centers
Use
School Libraries
Professional Concerns
NT Standards
Public Libraries
BT Libraries
Reference Service
BT Information Services
Referral Service
BT Information Services
School Libraries
BT Libraries
UF Media Centers
Special Libraries
BT Libraries
Staffing
NT Clerks
NT Librarians
NT Subprofessionals

Standards
  BT Professional Concerns
  RT Evaluation
Subprofessionals
  BT Staffing
University Libraries
  BT Academic Libraries

Extract of Subject Authority List (Hierarchical Arrangement)

Evaluation
- Accuracy
- Cost
- Timeliness

Information Services
- Interlibrary Loans
- Literature Searching
- Reference Service
- Referral Service

Libraries
- Academic Libraries
  - College Libraries
  - Junior College Libraries
  - University Libraries
- Public Libraries
- School Libraries
- Special Libraries

Professional Concerns
- Standards

Staffing
- Clerks
- Librarians
- Subprofessionals

SAMPLE QUERY: *Can clerks be used for answering reference queries?*

SEARCH STATEMENT: (Clerks *or* Staffing) *and* (Reference Service *or* Information Services).

Queries

1. References on cost of literature searches conducted in special libraries.
2. "What information services are offered in media centers?"
3. "I am interested in learning about personnel working in community college libraries."
4. Select documents on the evaluation of reference services.
5. "Are interlibrary loans being transacted between special libraries and media centers?"

Answers to Exercise 2 are on pp. 83–84.

ANSWERS

Exercise 1

1. Book lists
   Dartmouth Medal
   Encyclopedias and dictionaries
   Library resources
   McColvin Medal
   Publishers and publishing—reference books
   Reference books
   Research materials
   Special collections—directories
2. Book fairs
   Book week
   Broadsides
   Bulletin boards
   College and University libraries—exhibits and displays
   College and University libraries—services to the community
   Exhibits and displays
   Friends of the Library
   Historial libraries—exhibits and displays
   International Book Year 1972
   International Children's Book Day
   John Cotton Dana Library Public Relations Awards
   Library Community relations
   Library extension
   Library of Congress—exhibits and displays
   Library publications
   Library weeks and days
   National Library Week
   Posters
   Pressure groups in libraries
   Public libraries—exhibits and displays
   Public libraries—relations with local government
   Public relations of libraries
   Publicity
   School libraries—exhibits and displays
   Special libraries—exhibits and displays
   State libraries—exhibits and displays
   Survey—*Friends of the Library*

Exercise 2

1. (Cost *or* Evaluation) *and* (Literature Searching *or* Information Services) *and* (Special Libraries *or* Libraries).
2. (Information Services *or* Literature Searching *or* Reference Service *or* Referral Services *or* Interlibrary Loans) *and* (School Libraries *or* Libraries).

Note that Libraries is included as a generic descriptor in case there are references about information services in libraries related to but not specific as school libraries.

3. (Staffing *or* Clerks *or* Librarians *or* Subprofessionals) *and* (Junior College Libraries *or* Information Services).
4. Evaluation *or* Accuracy *or* Cost *or* Timeliness *or* Standards) *and* (Reference Service *or* Information Services).

   Observe that the more generic terms Staffing and Information Services are used to retrieve potentially relevant references on a topic.
5. This requires two search statements:

   1. (Interlibrary Loans *or* Information Services) *and* Special Libraries *and* School Libraries.
   2. (Interlibrary Loans *or* Information Services) *and* Libraries.

ADDITIONAL READING

Benson, James, and Maloney, Ruth Kay. "Principles of Searching." *RQ* **14** (1975):316–320.
Pope, Michael. "Subject Heading Muddle." *RQ* **15** (1975):129–131.

7

Answer Selection

A satisfactory answer to a reference query has two important characteristics: correctness and completeness. The *correctness* of an answer depends on its *accuracy*. A *complete* answer includes *all* essential information related to the query.

CORRECTNESS OF ANSWER

Correctness is the primary component of a satisfactory answer. An incorrect answer provided to an unknowing patron is useless, misleading, or even detrimental, depending on the way the requestor uses the information. Of course, no competent reference librarian would knowingly provide incorrect information, but it can be done inadvertently if both the reference librarian and the library user are unaware that the information provided is erroneous.

Data concerning the correctness of information provided by reference librarians have been gathered by Thomas Childers and Terence Crowley in an attempt to statistically report on the quality of library service. [1] Libraries in the study, unaware that their reference services were being investigated, were asked to provide answers to simple, short reference queries asked over the telephone. When the accuracy of the answers provided was analyzed, the percentage of correct answers ranged between 54 and 63%. This meant, of course, that about one-half of the answers given by the reference librarians in the sample were incorrect or only partially correct (in some instances, no answer was offered by the librarian at all). (A list of the queries asked in the study is given on pp. 108–110 in Childers' and Crowley's report.)

ERRORS IN STEPS OF THE REFERENCE PROCESS

Selection of an incorrect answer is influenced by a number of factors. The first group of factors resulting in incorrect answers are errors in any of the steps in the reference process that precede the answer selection step: message selection, negotiation, selection of tools to search, or selection of search headings within those tools.

If the message of the query is improperly selected (such as occurs when the librarian chooses an improper given or wanted descriptor), incorrect information results. In the query, "What does MARL mean?" the patron is asking for the meaning of the acronym *MARL* (Mobile Acoustics Research Laboratory). In this case the given descriptor for MARL is Abbreviation–Symbol. If the librarian incorrectly selects the given descriptor as Term–Subject, he or she will be seeking the definition of the word "marl" rather than the meaning of the acronym MARL. (It is important to remember that without proper negotiation the librarian may easily answer the wrong query or only part of the intended query. For instance, the patron who asks, "Which is the biggest airport in the U.S.?" may be defining *bigness* as number of take-offs and landings, square footage of terminal space, or size of landing area.)

Errors in the tool selection step also result in incorrect answers. Selection of unsatisfactory reference tools in which to search for an answer to a query is sometimes a result of prior errors in the message selection or negotiation steps. (However, it also occurs when these two previous steps are completed correctly.) In the query concerning the acronym MARL, the given descriptor, Term–Subject, could have been incorrectly selected instead of the correct one, Abbreviation–Symbol. Either of these descriptors would be a clue to search in the same *type* of tool—a dictionary. However, the specific tool selected in

[1] Childers, Thomas and Crowley, Terence. *Information Service in Public Libraries: Two Studies*. Metuchen, N. J.: Scarecrow Press, 1971. Pp. 139–141.

a search for an abbreviation or symbol (MARL) would be a dictionary of acronyms or abbreviations, whereas the tool selected in a search for the definition of a term (marl) would be a general language dictionary. In both of these types of dictionaries, a definition or description of the word could be found, but only one would be correct in relation to the query.

Once a specific title has been selected to search, errors in identification of access points within that tool also result in incorrect answers. The correct answer may actually be contained in the tool, but may be overlooked by a librarian who searches under subject headings that are too broad or too specific, or under terminology not used in that particular tool. For example, in response to a client request for "a book with illustrations showing how to trim a dog," the librarian may go directly to the card catalog to search under subject for possible titles. Without consulting the Library of Congress list of subject headings (or other authority list), the librarian might search under a series of incorrect subject headings: the general heading "Dogs" and the more specific headings "Dogs—Trimming" and "Dogs–Grooming." If the card catalog does not include "see" references to the appropriate subject heading, "Dog grooming," the librarian could overlook it entirely, informing the client that the library does not own any books specifically concerned with trimming dogs.

SELECTING AN ANSWER

After carefully and correctly completing message selection, negotiation, tool selection, and identification of access points within a reference tool, the librarian is ready to select an answer within that tool. Locating a title that contains the answer to a query, and even identifying the exact page on which that answer is located, is unfortunately no guarantee that a correct answer will be transmitted to the requestor. Many errors can occur in the process of selecting an answer and communicating it to the user. The most frequent cause of errors is misinterpretation of the information given in the answer-providing tool.

MISINTERPRETATION OF INFORMATION

Misinterpretation can occur when there are several closely related answers presented in the reference source. For instance, a reference tool searched for data on the number of single men in the U.S. may present data in terms of both "single" and "formerly married" males. In order to determine which of these terms is used in the sense intended by the patron (based on pre-search negotiation with the patron), the reference source should be searched for a satisfactory explanation of these terms. Making a guess about which of the terms is most suitable without looking for explanations or notes in the tool may result in misinterpretation of the data provided, and an incorrect answer.

Misinterpretation of the information given in a reference source can also occur when the information given is not presented exactly according to the requirements of the query, requiring interpretation or translation of the information into a suitable form. For example, in a search for data on the number of gallons of petroleum produced in the U.S. by offshore drilling, the librarian may locate an answer stated in terms of barrels rather than gallons. If postsearch negotiation with the requestor indicates that gallons is the preferred answer, the librarian must go one step further and locate information on how to convert barrels to gallons in order to provide a correct

No. 57. FAMILIES, BY CHARACTERISTICS: 1974

[Number in thousands. As of March. Based on Current Population Survey; includes members of the Armed Forces liv off post or with their families on post, but excludes all other members of the Armed Forces; see text, p. 1. For definit of families, see text, p. 3]

Characteristic	All families		Male head: Married, wife present		Male head: Other marital status		Female head		Families of negro and other place	
	Number	Percent	Number	Percent	Number	Percent	Number	Percent	Number	Perc
All families	55,053	100.0	46,812	100.0	1,438	100.0	6,804	100.0	6,134	10
White	48,919	88.9	42,894	91.6	1,172	81.5	4,853	71.3	(X)	(
Negro and other	6,134	11.1	3,918	8.4	265	18.4	1,951	28.7	6,134	10
Size of family:										
2 persons	20,592	37.4	16,654	35.6	881	61.3	3,057	44.9	1,816	2
3 persons	11,673	21.2	9,718	20.8	291	20.3	1,663	24.4	1,332	2
4 persons	10,789	19.6	9,721	20.8	120	8.4	947	13.9	1,114	1
5 persons	6,386	11.6	5,745	12.3	82	5.7	559	8.2	733	[illegible]
6 persons	3,021	5.5	2,700	5.8	44	3.0	278	4.1	471	
7 or more persons	2,593	4.7	2,273	4.9	19	1.3	300	4.4	668	[illegible]
Own children under age 18:										
None	25,303	46.0	21,534	46.0	1,047	72.8	2,722	40.0	2,310	
1	10,586	19.2	8,761	18.7	204	14.2	1,621	23.8	1,281	
2	9,865	17.9	8,565	18.3	95	6.6	1,204	17.7	1,031	
3	5,246	9.5	4,591	9.8	42	2.9	612	9.0	677	
4 or more	4,052	7.4	3,360	7.2	50	3.5	644	9.5	835	
Own children under age 6:										
None	41,301	75.0	34,731	74.2	1,365	94.9	5,206	76.5	4,215	
1	9,286	16.9	8,094	17.3	59	4.1	1,133	16.7	1,266	
2	3,749	6.8	3,376	7.2	9	0.7	364	5.3	498	
3 or more	716	1.3	610	1.3	5	0.3	101	1.5	153	

X Not applicable

Source: U.S. Bureau of the Census, *Current Population Reports*, series P-20, No.276.

FIGURE 7-1. Source: Table from *Statistical Abstract of the United States*, 96th ed. Washington, D.C.: U.S. Department of Commerce, 1975. P. 43.

TABLE SAMPLE QUERY: *How many white families were headed by females in 1974?*
ANSWER: 4,853,000 families.
Qualifications: As of March 1974, includes members of the Armed Forces living off post or with their families on post, but excludes all other members of the Armed Forces.
Source: U.S. Bureau of the Census, *Current Population Reports, Series P. 20*, No. 276.
Citation: *Statistical Abstract of the United States*. 96th ed. Washington, D.C.: U.S. Department of Commerce, 1975. P. 43.

answer. The preceding example raises another problem: the hazards of misinterpretation when the librarian must interpret data presented in the pictoral or tabular form of a table, graph, or chart. Robert Fairthorne, a mathematician interested in problems of librarianship, once stated that librarians are typically literate rather than numerate. He based this opinion on observations, confirmed by others, that most librarians have backgrounds in the humanities and social sciences rather than mathematics or science. However, in selecting answers to some queries, a reference librarian needs elementary mathematical skills. Specifically, he or she needs to be able to select answers from data (numbers with assigned meaning) presented in graphic form. Such queries are asked in *all* types of libraries and not just in science and technology libraries.

In some cases the patron will expect the librarian to merely locate a graphic presentation of the requested information, preferring to personally select the answer from the graph. But frequently the patron will require the librarian's assistance in selecting a correct answer from the data presented. In the section that follows, the four kinds of graphic presentations that you are likely to encounter—tables, line graphs, bar graphs, and circle graphs—are defined and discussed.

Tables

Tables provide a systematic arrangement of data in either columns or rows. (An example of a table is provided in Figure 7-1.)

Line Graphs

Line graphs show how quantities (for example, income or expenditure) vary over time or over other variables. (Figure 7-2 provides an example of a line graph.)

RESEARCH AND DEVELOPMENT FUNDS,
BY PERFORMANCE SECTOR AND SOURCE: 1960 to 1975

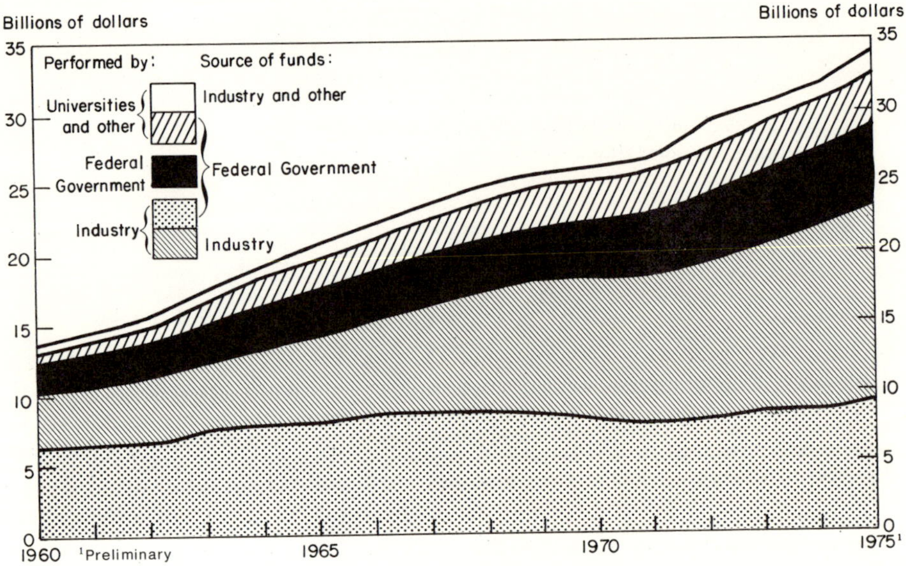

FIGURE 7-2. Source: Line graph adapted from *Statistical Abstract of the United States*, 96th ed. Washington, D.C.: U.S. Department of Commerce, 1975. P. 547.

LINE GRAPH SAMPLE QUERY: *Was 1963 the year of highest expenditure for research sponsored by the federal government?*

ANSWER: No. If you draw a line at a right angle to the data line (labeled 1960–1975) from the point beginning with 1963, that line will intersect the curve at a point below its peak. The peak represents the year with the highest ex-expenditure. Therefore, 1963 was not the year most money was spent for research.

Source: U.S. Bureau of the Census.

Citation: *Statistical Abstract of the United States*; 96th ed. Washington, D.C.: U.S. Department of Commerce, 1975. P. 547.

Bar Graphs

Bar graphs provide comparisons between data—for example, average cost of periodical subscriptions during different years. The bars may be depicted vertically or horizontally. Note that the same date may be presented

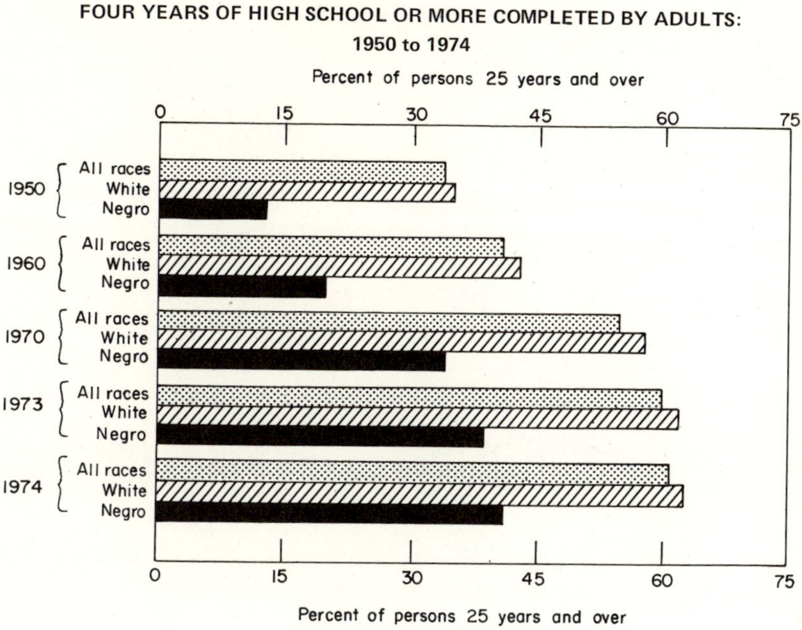

FIGURE 7-3. Bar graph. Source: Adapted from *Statistical Abstract of the United States*, 96th ed. Washington, D.C.: U.S. Department of Commerce, 1975. P. 109.

BAR GRAPH SAMPLE QUERY: *What percentage of all persons 25 years or over had 4 years of high school or more education in 1960?*

ANSWER: About 40%. Take the bar marked "All races" for 1960 and measure its length on the percentage scale at the base of the graph. The bar ends about two-thirds of the distance between 30 and 45%, hence, the answer is approximately 40%.

Source: U.S. Bureau of the Census.

Citation: *Statistical Abstract of the United States.*, 96th ed. Washington, D.C.: U.S. Department of Commerce, 1975. P. 109.

either as a table or a line graph, or a bar graph. (Figure 7-3 depicts a bar graph.)

Circle Graphs

Circle graphs, sometimes called pie charts, show how data are divided among component parts (how the pie is cut up). (Figure 7-4 provides an example of a circle graph.)

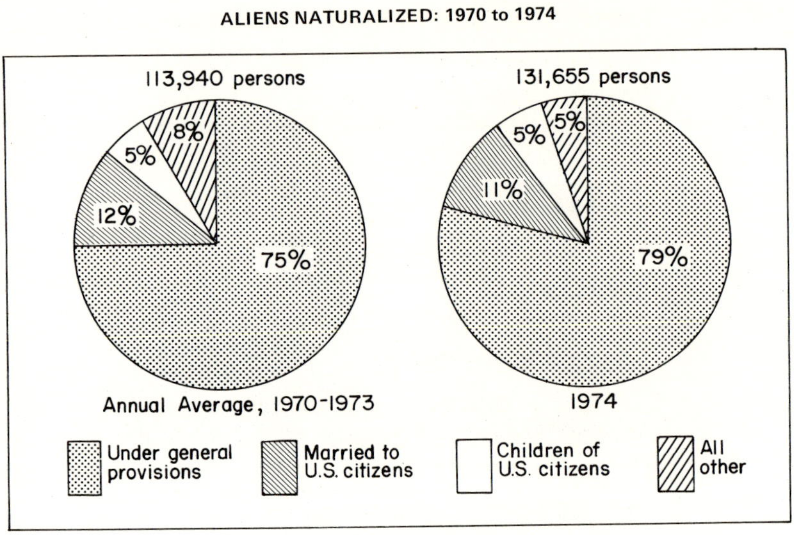

FIGURE 7-4. Circle graph. Source: Adapted from *Statistical Abstract of the United States*; 96th ed. Washington, D.C.: U.S. Department of Commerce, 1975. P. 96.

CIRCLE GRAPH SAMPLE QUERY: *What percentage of aliens were naturalized in 1974 as a result of being children of U.S. citizens?*

ANSWER: 5% of persons naturalized in 1974.

Source: U.S. Immigration and Naturalization Service.

Citation: *Statistical Abstract of the United States*. 96th ed. Washington, D.C.: U.S. Department of Commerce, 1975. P. 96.

You may be asked to take the preceding sample query a step further by giving the number of people so naturalized. The total number of naturalized citizens for 1974 is 131,655 (given on the chart), and 5% of that would be 6582. Because 5% is $\frac{1}{20}$ of 100%, this answer can be obtained by either dividing 131,655 by 20 or multiplying 131,655 by 0.05. Disregard numbers to the right of the decimal point. Fractions should not be counted when the calculations represent numbers of people.

Guidelines for Selecting Answers from Graphs

Graphs are used to present information in a concise form. As the old saying goes, a picture is worth a thousand words. A few guidelines for selecting answers from graphs follow.

1. *Read* the heading and explanatory notes *before* selecting information from the graph. This is essential to the selection of a correct answer from the graph.

2. Select the answer from the correct portion of the graph. Avoid errors in copying numbers. It is good practice to double-check your answers when you have recorded them to insure that the information has been copied from the correct portion of the graph and to avoid errors of number transposition.

3. If the desired answer is not given on the graph a "near" answer may be acceptable. (For example, if the average cost of books published in the U.S. during the last year is not included in the graph, supply the latest cost given in the graph).

4. Qualify the numeric answer with all of the necessary information given in the graph. This includes information in the heading as well as explanatory notes that may be anywhere in the graph. For example, if the temperature during a given month in a particular city is requested, copy the unit of measurement—degrees Fahrenheit or Celsius—whether it is the average, high, or low temperature. Also copy where the temperature was recorded, and any other qualifications given in the graph.

5. Give the original source of information when possible. The source of the graph is the individual or agency responsible for the collection of the data, for example, the U.S. Bureau of the Census. The original source is not always indicated in the answer-providing tool, but when given it usually appears under the chart heading, or as a footnote. When a graph has been reproduced from another tool, a citation may be given, providing the document from which the information has been reproduced—for example, in *Statistical Abstract of the U.S.* The patron may want to refer back to the original source for further information, or to consider it in determining the reliability of the data in the reproduced graph.

6. In some cases, numbers on the graph require conversion. For example, a percentage figure might have to be converted into a number of units. This is done by simple multiplication or division, for example,

conversion of 20% of 4000 into number of units by either (a) multiplication of 4000 by which equals $0.2 \neq 800$ or (b) division of 4000 by $5 = 800$.

Another example of conversion of percentage figure into number of units is given with the sample query for Figure 7-4.

NO ANSWER

Occasionally, the correct answer to a query is that no answer is available, either in your library collection or in the literature. In the case of complicated or obscure queries, your library's reference collection may not include the type of tools necessary to provide an answer. If you cannot locate the answer in your own library but believe it may be available through other sources, you should refer the user to the library service or community information source likely to have access to an answer. Your referral should include complete information, including the name of the individual or organization to contact, as well as address, telephone number, and hours of service. If you are referring the user to a local information source, it is advisable to telephone first to ensure the source will be able to help and to alert them that the patron will be contacting them.

At times, a thorough search will convince you that no answer to the query has been documented in the literature. When this occurs, the correct answer to the query is that there is no answer available. (This may be a very desirable response to a researcher planning to investigate a certain topic and hoping that the idea has not already been explored by someone else.) Other patrons with other information needs may be disappointed that no answer can be identified in the literature. In all such cases, your negative answer should include a complete list of the sources and search headings you checked without success. If, at a later date, the patron decides to continue the search on his or her own or to seek help from another library, your steps will not have to be repeated.

COMPLETENESS OF ANSWER

A complete answer to a query is one which provides all possible correct answers, as well as interpretation or explanation of the answer when needed, and documentation for the source in which the answer was found.

Providing All Correct Answers

Providing all possible correct answers for a query may mean giving more information than was actually requested. A patron may make an assumption about the size or form of the answer expected by the way he or she phrases the query to the librarian. For example, a request for "the title and author of the biography of Dwight D. Eisenhower," indicates only one such biography has been written. In actuality, your search may reveal that several biographies have been written about Dwight D. Eisenhower. A complete answer would be one that informs the library user of biographies available, offering bibliographic information about each of them.

Occasionally, the number of possible answers to what appears to be a simple factual query proves to be greater than either the librarian or the requestor anticipated. In a case like this, it is probably best to renegotiate the user's information request in light of the new knowledge you have gained about the information, a technique called "post search negotiation." This will make possible the selection of the most suitable answer or answers from numerous possible answers. For example, a request for the name and address of a manufacturer of baseball equipment could result in the names of dozens of companies. At this point, the librarian should explain that there are several possible answers, and attempt to redefine the query by asking the client whether he is interested in manufacturers in a certain state or region of the country, or whether any other limits can be placed on the answer. Often it will be a surprise to the client that many possible answers exist and it will be a simple matter to work with him to narrow the request. (Post search negotiation will be discussed more thoroughly in Chapter 8 on "Query Negotiation.")

Providing a complete answer also involves anticipation of information not specifically requested in the original query, but which the client might need. A common example of this occurs with clients' telephone queries asking whether the library owns a particular book. If the answer is yes, at least two additional queries can be predicted: "Is the book checked out?" and "What is the call number?" In checking the card catalog to determine whether the library owns an item, an experienced reference librarian will note additional information that might be helpful to the user or requested by the user once he or she is sure the library owns the material. This additional information could include bibliographic information, the call number, and, if it can be conveniently checked, the availability of the item.

Another example of anticipating further information needs is with requests for names of individuals or organizations. Even though the request may be only for the name of the person or organization, users frequently want or can use addresses and phone numbers in addition. It is more efficient in the long run to collect the complete information in your initial search and offer it to the user, even though it was not specifically requested.

Currency is also a component of a complete answer. It is sometimes tempting to limit the answer to the scope available in the answer-providing title. For instance, a request for the number of best-selling novels written by a particular author could be partially answered using a reference source, such as an almanac, which lists best sellers for the last 50 years. Such lists usually include a note concerning the cutoff date for inclusion, often several months prior to publication of the tool. This can result in a gap of several months between the time the list was compiled and published and the time you are searching for information. Your answer to this query would not be complete until additional sources had been checked, to verify the answer up to the current date.

Explanation and Interpretation of the Answer

Some answers require explanation or interpretation by the librarian before they are complete. Queries answered with numbers or statistics, for instance, typically require qualification. If a library user asks about "the temperature in Miami, Florida in the winter," 59° is an incomplete answer for several reasons. First, you would need to indicate the unit of measurement: 59° Celsius (°C) or Fahrenheit (°F). You should also carefully read and explain any notes and explanations in the answer-providing title which may clarify whether 59° is the high, low, or average temperature, and for which month or months it was recorded.

Although explanation and interpretation are considered important aspects of a complete answer to general types of queries, special caution should be exercised in providing answers for legal or medical queries. In many cases it is possible to provide information for legal or medical queries just as you would for any other type of query, by referring the patron to relevant information contained in an appropriate answer-providing title. Occasionally, however, a user comes to the library seeking solutions to complex legal or medical problems which require the professional services of a doctor or lawyer, and cannot be solved by a simple referral to written documents. For example, the individual who plans to act as his own attorney in court may begin by requesting state statutes regarding certain aspects of the law, as well as references to related court decisions. Once the librarian has provided the texts of the law and court decisions, the user may discover that the material is too complicated for a layman to understand. At this point he may pressure the librarian to explain or interpret the information in the answer-providing tool. Similar requests can result when an untrained individual is attempting to understand information in medical resources.

As a librarian you should never attempt to provide legal or medical advice to a client, or to interpret the implications of legal or medical statements in reference sources. The reference librarian is expected to retrieve information stored in library resources, completely and correctly, but not to become involved in the use or interpretation of this information by the requestor. A librarian should seek to impartially locate and provide information within the scope of the library's reference collection, but to limit explanations or interpretations of legal or medical material to those dealing with proper use of the answer-providing tool.

Postsearch Negotiation

A reference source may not provide information in the exact form in which it was requested. If the user asks for the temperature in Miami in the winter, and the answer listed is for the month of January alone, you would need to point this out in transmitting the answer to the user. The temperature for the month of January alone may be completely satisfactory for the requestor's needs, or he or she may clarify the original query by explaining that he or she really wants a single average temperature for the period between November and February. In a case such as this, you and the client are engaging in postsearch negotiation, renegotiating the query after an answer has been found. The possibility that follow-up negotiation will be necessary after the completion of your search is not unusual, since neither the librarian nor the client can always predict what the search will reveal. You should attempt, however, to determine all that the client can tell you about the query in the pre-search negotiation stage.

Level of Information Desired

One factor in determining the complete answer to a query is the amount and level of information desired by the requestor. Some queries, such as a request for a business address, have one and only one possible answer. Others, requests for background information on a subject, for example, have many possible correct answers. You should identify the amount and level of information desired by the user in pre-search negotiation. For instance, a request for information on the life cycle of the ant has numerous possible correct answers, ranging from the basic information presented in an encyclopedia to technical or research data available in scientific journals. In negotiation you should pinpoint the scope of the answer desired by the client, and use this knowledge to determine when you have provided a complete answer. You should neither overwhelm the user with correct but extraneous, unneeded information, nor shortchange the user with a less complete answer than requested.

Documentation of the Answer

Another component of a complete answer is the documentation of the source of the answer. Whenever you provide a client with an answer to a query, you should also offer information concerning where you located the answer, whether it is requested or not. This is a good reference practice for several reasons. First of all, it shows the client that the information a reference librarian provides is based on skill in retrieving information stored in library or community resources. Second, it performs an instructional function by acquainting library users with specific reference sources and types of information these sources provide. Finally, it clarifies the responsibility for the ultimate authority of the answer as being that of the answer-providing tool. This is especially important when the user has requested information in the form of recommendations or evaluations of products or other materials. The librarian should emphasize to the user that the evaluation provided is not based on the personal opinion of the librarian, but has been retrieved from the cited reference source.

The amount of documentation you provide to a user depends on that user's needs, but the minimum amount of bibliographic information you should offer is the title of the answer-providing tool. If the user is not in the library with you when you locate an answer, record the complete citation of the source in case it is requested. The record of the citation should be complete and unambiguous to allow you or anyone else to trace the source of your answer without difficulty. A complete bibliographic citation for a book typically consists of the author(s), title, place of publication, publisher, year of publication, edition, volume (in case of multivolume sets), and the specific page or pages on which the answer is located. If the book is paginated by sections rather than continuously, you should also provide the section number. For journal articles, a complete citation consists of the authors(s) of the article, the title of the article, the journal title and volume number, the publication date, and the complete pagination. For a journal, a complete and unambiguous citation may also require the series number, and issue number if each issue is paginated separately (otherwise there may be, for example, 12 pages numbered 21 in a given year).

SUMMARY

In this chapter we have discussed a crucial step in the reference process, that of answer selection. Many possible errors can occur in this step, resulting in an unsatisfactory answer to a requestor's query. A satisfactory answer should be both correct and complete. Some of the possible errors include misinterpretation of information, failure to fully circumscribe an answer, and failure to locate the most current answer available.

QUESTIONS FOR DISCUSSION

Give an example in which an answer provided for a query might be correct, but not complete.

What steps can a librarian take to guard against misinterpretation of the information given in a reference tool?

Should the librarian be held responsible when the information cited in a reference title turns out to be incorrect?

What are some reasons that a librarian may be unable to locate an answer for a query in the reference sources available in his or her library?

What is the nature of legal and medical queries, and the legal and medical literature, that influence the scope of answers provided by a librarian for those subject areas?

EXERCISE: Answer Selection

(Use the tables or charts that follow each query to determine the answer to the query.)

1. *Query*: How much has the weekly grocery bill increased for a family of four (with two children under age 5) since 1965?"

   a. $20.20
   b. $28.10
   c. $49.60
   d. $17.40

Answer: ______________

No. **691.** Weekly Food Cost for Families, by Type of Family: 1965 to 1974

[**In dollars.** As of December. Based on moderate-cost food plan; assumes all meals are eaten at home or taken from home]

FAMILY TYPE	1965	1967	1968	1969	1970	1971	1972	1973	1974
Couple, 20–35 years old	20.20	20.80	21.60	23.10	23.20	24.20	25.40	30.80	34.40
Couple, 55–75 years old	17.20	17.60	17.90	19.40	19.40	20.20	21.20	25.70	28.40
Couple with children:									
1 child, 1–5 years old	25.10	25.80	26.80	28.70	28.80	30.00	31.40	38.20	42.50
1 child, 15–18 years old	29.30	29.90	30.90	33.30	33.30	35.00	36.60	44.40	49.40
2 children, 1–5 years old	29.40	30.30	31.40	33.60	33.70	35.10	36.80	44.70	49.60
2 children, 6–11 years old	34.00	35.00	36.40	39.10	39.20	40.90	42.90	52.00	58.10
2 children, 12–18 years old	37.50	38.40	39.80	42.90	42.90	44.90	47.10	57.10	63.60

Source: U.S. Agricultural Research Service, unpublished data.

(The preceding table is from *Statistical Abstract of the United States*, 96th ed. Washington, D.C.: U.S. Department of Commerce, 1975. P. 425.)

2. *Query*: "By about what percentage did domestic waterborne commerce increase during the years 1950–1970?

   a. About 3000%
   b. About 46%
   c. About 33%
   d. About 20%

Answer: ______________

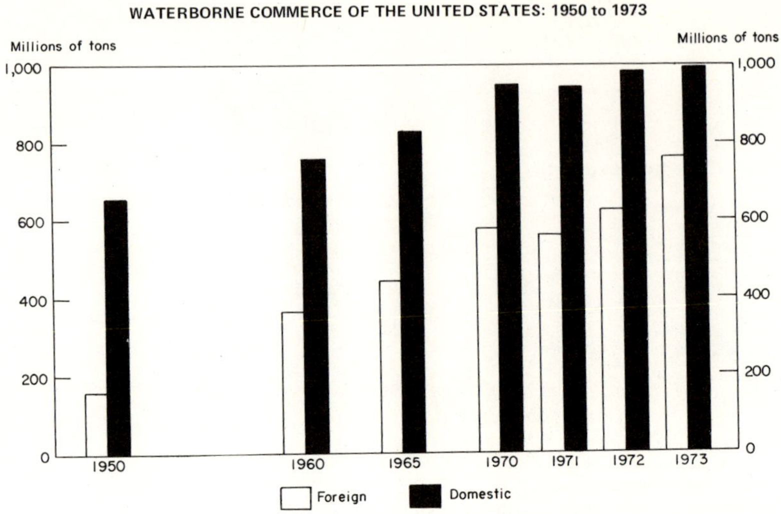

(The preceding bar graph is adapted from *Statistical Abstract of the United States*, 96th ed. Washington, D.C.: U.S. Department of Commerce, 1975. P. 589.)

3. *Query*: "Property taxes represent what percentage of a state's revenue?"

   a. 2.1%
   b. 21%
   c. 79%
   d. 18%

Answer: ____________________

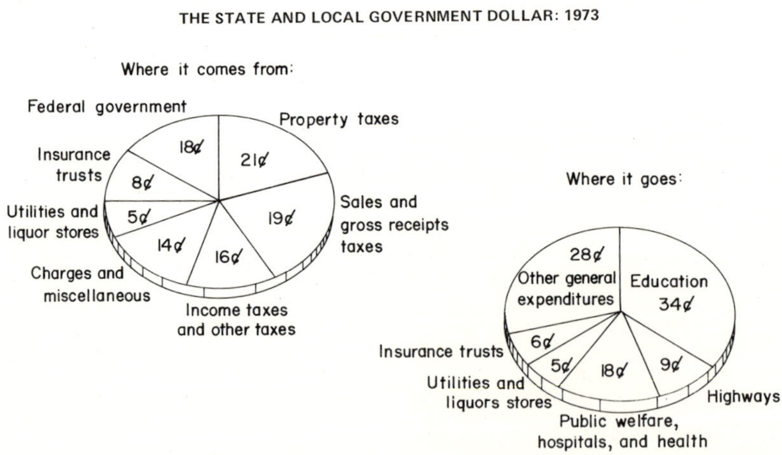

(The preceding circle graph is adapted from *Statistical Abstract of the United States*, 96th ed. Washington, D.C.: U.S. Department of Commerce, 1975. P. 248.)

4. *Query*: "In 1974, what was the least expensive metropolitan area in which a retired couple could live?"

a. Austin, Texas
b. Baton Rouge La
c. Baltimore, Md.
d. Dallas, Texas

Answer: ____________________

No. **694.** Urban Intermediate Budget for a 4-Person Family and a Retired Couple—Total Cost, 1967 to 1974, and for Selected Metropolitan Areas: 1974

[**In dollars, except percent.** Based on autumn prices. **4**-person family budget refers to annual cost at an intermediate level of living for a family comprising a 38-year-old employed husband, wife not employed outside the home, 8-year-old girl, and 13-year-old boy; retired couple refers to a husband age 65 or over and his wife]

AREA	COST FOR 4-PERSON FAMILY					COST FOR RETIRED COUPLE				
	Total	Food	Housing[1]	Transportation	Other[2]	Total	Food	Housing[1]	Transportation	Other[2]
1967, Urban U.S	9,076	2,105	2,230	892	3,849	3,857	1,048	1,330	382	1,097
Percent	100.0	23.2	24.6	9.8	42.4	100.0	27.2	34.5	9.9	28.4
1970, Urban U.S	10,664	2,452	2,501	912	4,799	4,489	1,220	1,554	413	1,302
Percent	100.0	23.0	23.5	8.6	45.0	100.0	27.2	34.6	9.2	29.0
1972, Urban U.S	11,446	2,673	2,810	979	4,984	[3]4,776	[3]1,255	[3]1,673	[3]438	[3]1,410
Percent	100.0	23.4	24.6	8.6	43.0	[3]100.0	[3]26.3	[3]35.0	[3]9.2	[3]29.5
1973, Urban U.S	12,626	3,183	2,908	1,014	5,521	[4]4,967	[4]1,328	[4]1,745	[4]448	[4]1,446
Percent	100.00	25.2	23.0	8.0	43.7	[4]100.0	[4]26.7	[4]35.2	[4]9.0	[4]29.1
1974, Urban U.S	**14,333**	**3,548**	**3,236**	**1,171**	**6,378**	[5]**5,414**	[5]**1,599**	[5]**1,839**	[5]**462**	[5]**1,514**
Percent	100.0	24.8	22.6	8.2	44.5	[5]100.0	[5]29.5	[5]34.0	[5]8.5	[5]28.0
Nonmetropolitan areas[6]	12,945	3,321	2,828	1,158	5,638	4,746	1,536	1,397	439	1,374
Metropolitan areas[7]	14,644	3,599	3,327	1,174	6,544	5,637	1,620	1,986	469	1,562
Atlanta, Ga	13,098	3,444	2,615	1,165	5,874	5,005	1,569	1,439	481	1,516
Austin, Tex	12,388	3,147	2,472	1,218	5,551	4,914	1,449	1,500	486	1,479
Bakersfield, Calif	13,000	3,235	2,674	1,192	5,899	5,161	1,489	1,684	491	1,497
Baltimore, Md	14,398	3,471	2,927	1,167	6,833	5,287	1,553	1,683	507	1,544
Baton Rouge, La	12,928	3,464	2,627	1,171	5,666	4,788	1,583	1,283	488	1,434
Bostin, Mass	16,725	3,829	4,458	1,181	7,257	6,415	1,744	2,626	434	1,611
Buffalo, N.Y	15,364	3,667	3,522	1,267	6,908	5,916	1,659	2,124	555	1,578
Cedar Rapids, Iowa	14,092	3,151	3,198	1,197	6,546	5,360	1,466	1,862	486	1,546
Champaign-Urbana, Ill	14,587	3,425	3,441	1,202	6,519	5,620	1,585	1,949	490	1,596
Chicago, Ill.-Northwestern Indiana	14,797	3,563	3,492	1,215	6,527	5,538	1,618	1,906	441	1,573
Cincinnati, Ohio-Ky.-Ind	13,753	3,525	2,988	1,206	6,034	5,111	1,563	1,581	480	1,487
Cleveland, Ohio	14,617	3,463	3,488	1,203	6,463	5,577	1,548	1,942	529	1,558
Dallas, Tex	12,917	3,200	2,732	1,226	5,759	5,025	1,431	1,587	504	1,503
Dayton, Ohio	13,391	3,519	2,825	1,154	5,893	5,158	1,559	1,622	483	1,494
Denver, Colo	13,606	3,374	2,804	1,154	6,274	5,260	1,527	1,711	489	1,533
Detroit, Mich	14,390	3,594	3,251	1,162	6,383	5,484	1,639	1,783	510	1,552
Durham, N.C	13,927	3,382	2,990	1,127	6,428	5,140	1,519	1,645	479	1,497
Green Bay, Wis	14,180	3,167	3,219	1,165	6,629	5,273	1,462	1,795	480	1,536
Hartford, Conn	15,501	3,841	3,804	1,304	6,552	6,170	1,745	2,195	563	1,667
Honolulu, Hawaii	17,019	4,150	4,070	1,307	7,492	6,038	1,834	1,996	626	1,582
Houston, Tex	12,872	3,403	2,605	1,195	5,669	5,039	1,527	1,532	498	1,482
Indianapolis, Ind	14,120	3,393	3,199	1,297	6,231	5,554	1,558	1,923	529	1,544
Kansas City, Mo.-Kans	13,939	3,531	2,894	1,250	6,264	5,416	1,579	1,743	523	1,571
Lancaster, Pa	14,130	3,715	2,964	1,167	6,284	5,313	1,637	1,687	486	1,503
Los Angeles-Long Beach, Calif	14,068	3,387	3,111	1,192	6,378	5,496	1,506	1,899	535	1,556
Milwaukee, Wis	15,024	3,301	3,526	1,173	7,024	5,487	1,490	1,941	517	1,539
Minneapolis-St. Paul, Minn	14,917	3,429	3,082	1,168	7,238	5,444	1,542	1,846	499	1,557
Nashville, Tenn	12,996	3,241	2,883	1,172	5,700	5,199	1,489	1,672	495	1,543
New York, N.Y.-Northeastern N.J	16,648	4,099	4,072	1,085	7,392	6,353	1,822	2,563	344	1,624
Orlando, Fla	12,804	3,240	2,809	1,158	5,597	5,055	1,431	1,672	480	1,472
Philadelphia, Pa.-N.J	14,757	3,896	3,095	1,107	6,659	5,668	1,731	1,995	405	1,537
Pittsburgh, Pa	13,876	3,669	2,853	1,130	6,224	5,446	1,649	1,769	501	1,527
Portland, Maine	14,697	3,768	3,420	1,219	6,290	5,625	1,694	1,904	502	1,525
St. Louis, Mo.-Ill	13,859	3,570	2,997	1,247	6,045	5,375	1,617	1,721	556	1,481
San Diego, Calif	13,977	3,323	3,062	1,238	6,354	5,304	1,470	1,810	510	1,514

(*continued*)

4. *Query* (*continued*)

San Francisco-Oakland, Calif	15,127	3,528	3,593	1,225	6,781	5,919	1,557	2,145	565	1,652
Seattle-Everett, Wash	14,487	3,587	3,450	1,201	6,249	5,724	1,615	2,030	499	1,580
Washington, D.C.-Md.-Va	15,035	3,671	3,354	1,211	6,799	5,618	1,656	1,877	522	1,563
Wichita, Kans	13,302	3,302	2,836	1,194	5,970	5,200	1,482	1,730	493	1,495

[1] Includes weighted average cost of renter and homeowner shelter, housefurnishings, and household operations.
[2] Includes medical care, clothing and personal care, other family consumption, gifts and contributions, personal income taxes (except for retired couple in 1973), and, for 4-person families, also basic life insurance, occupational expenses, and social security.
[3] 1971 data. [4] 1972 data. [5] 1973 data.
[6] Places with population of 2,500–50,000 in 1960.
[7] For components, see U.S. Office of Management and Budget, "Standard Metropolitan Statistical Areas, 1967."

Source: U.S. Bureau of Labor Statistics, *Autumn 1974 Urban Family Budgets and Geographical Comparative Indexes* (Supplement to Bulletin 1570–5) and *3 Budgets for a Retired Couple, Autumn 1973* (Supplement to Bulletin 1570–6).

(The preceding table is from *Statistical Abstract of the United States*, 96th ed. Washington, D.C.: U.S. Department of Commerce, 1975. P. 427)

5. *Query*: "What has been the percentage of increase in total expenditures on education since 1960?"

   a. About 85%
   b. About 100%
   c. About 275%
   d. About 340%

Answer: ____________________

PUBLIC AND PRIVATE SCHOOL ENROLLMENT AND EXPENDITURES: 1960 to 1975

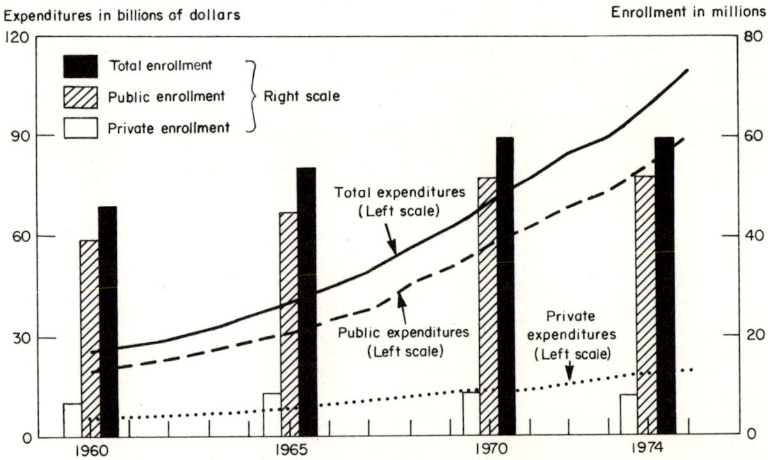

(The preceding graph is adapted from *Statistical Abstract of the United States*, 96th ed. Washington, D.C.: U.S. Department of Commerce, 1975. P. 109)

6. *Query*: What is the current rate of suicide in the U.S.?

   a. 13 per 100,000
   b. 15 per 100,000
   c. 16 per 100,000
   d. 29 per 100,000

Answer: ____________________

HOMICIDE AND SUICIDE RATES: 1965 to 1973

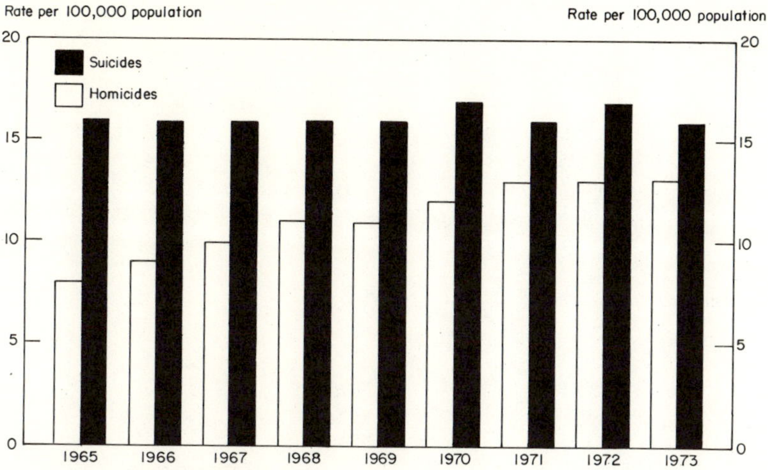

(The preceding graph is adapted from *Statistical Abstract of the United States*, 96th ed. Washington, D.C.: U.S. Department of Commerce, 1975. P. 149)

7. *Query*: "Approximately how many people traveled on airlines in the United States during 1970?"

   a. 150 million
   b. 7 million
   c. 1600 million
   d. Answer cannot be determined from graph

Answer: ____________________

DOMESTIC SCHEDULED AIR CARRIERS – REVENUES, MILES FLOWN, AND PASSENGERS CARRIED: 1960 to 1973

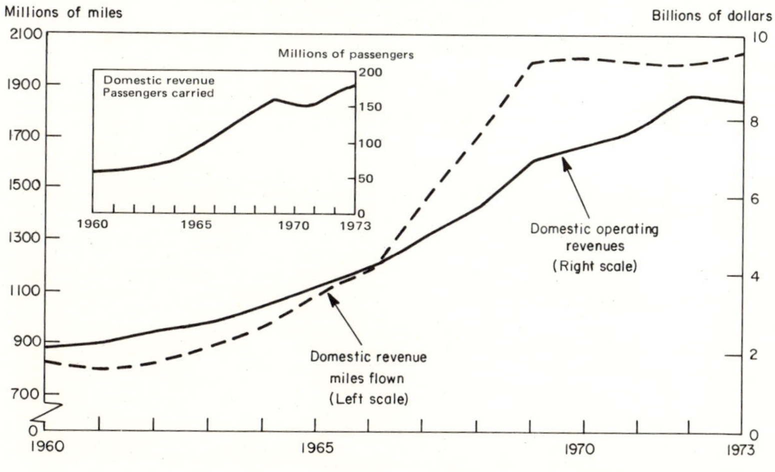

(The preceding line graph is adapted from *Statistical Abstract of the United States*, 96th ed. Washington, D.C.: U.S. Department of Commerce, 1975. P. 589.)

8. *Query*: "About how many farms were there in the United States in 1974 compared with 1950?"

a. 2.7 million more
b. 5 million more
c. 3 million less
d. 1.3 million less

Answer: ____________________

CHANGES IN FARMING: 1940 to 1974

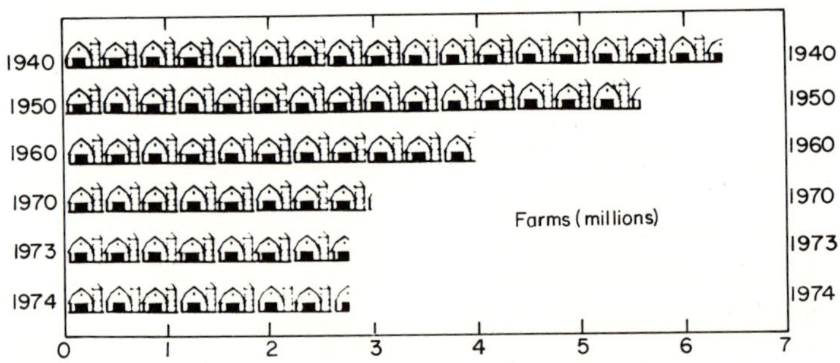

(The preceding chart is adapted from *Statistical Abstract of the United States*, 96th ed. Washington, D.C.: U.S. Department of Commerce, 1975. P. 824.)

9. *Query*: "The birth rate in Puerto Rico declined during the years 1965 to 1973 by what percentage?"

a. 7%
b. 17%
c. 23%
d. 29%

Answer: ____________________

BIRTH AND DEATH RATES FOR PUERTO RICO: 1965 to 1973
(Rate per 1000 population)

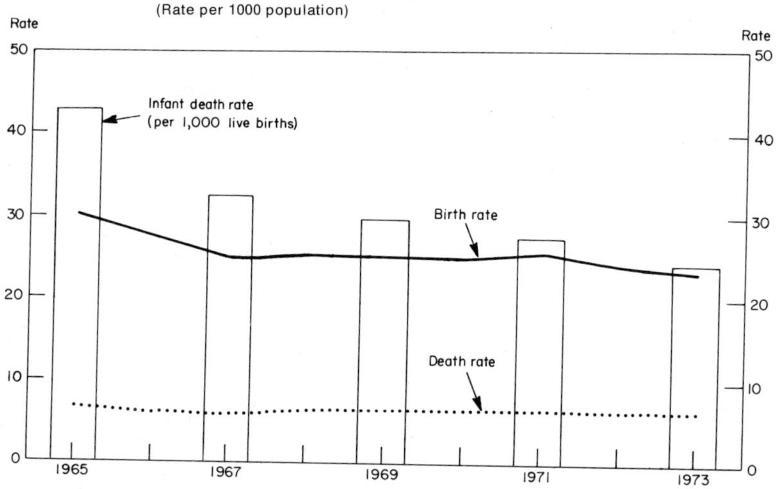

(The preceding graph is adapted from *Statistical Abstract of the United States*, 96th ed. Washington, D.C.: U.S. Department of Commerce, 1975. P. 824.)

10. *Query*: "How many more married women are there presently in the U.S. labor force than were employed in 1950?"

    a. 12,561
    b. 21,111,000
    c. 12,561,000
    d. 1,256,100

Answer: ____________

No. **565.** Married Women (Husband Present) in the Labor Force, by Age and Presence of Children: 1950 to 1975

[In thousands, **except percent!** As of March, except 1955 (Apr.). Prior to 1960, excludes Alaska and Hawaii. See also *Historical Statistics, Colonial Times to 1970*, series D 63–74]

ITEM	1950	1955	1960	1965	1970	1972[1]	1973[1]	1974[1]	1975[1]
Married women, husband present	**8,550**	**10,423**	**12,253**	**14,708**	**18,377**	**19,249**	**19,821**	**20,367**	**21,111**
With no children under 18 yr. old	4,946	5,227	5,692	6,755	8,174	8,797	9,107	9,365	9,702
With children 6–17 yr. old only	2,205	3,183	4,087	4,836	6,289	6,706	6,658	6,792	6,972
With children under 6 yr. old	1,399	2,012	2,474	3,117	3,914	3,746	4,056	4,210	4,437
Also with children 6–17 yr. old	651	1,086	1,351	1,709	2,040	1,73	1,786	1,867	1,934
PERCENT LABOR FORCE PARTICIPATION[2]									
Married women, husband present	**23.8**	**27.7**	**30.5**	**34.7**	**40.8**	**41.5**	**42.2**	**43.0**	**44.4**
With no children under 18 yr. old	30.3	32.7	34.7	38.3	42.2	42.7	42.8	43.0	43.9
With children 6–17 yr. old only	28.3	34.7	39.0	42.7	49.2	50.2	50.1	51.2	52.4
With children under 6 yr. old	11.9	16.2	18.6	23.3	30.3	30.1	32.7	34.4	36.6
Also with children 6–17 yr. old	12.6	17.3	18.9	22.8	30.5	29.1	30.9	32.9	34.3

[1] 1972–1975 data not comparable with earlier years due to the use of 1970 census data in estimation procedure.
[2] Married women in the labor force as percent of married women in the population.

(The preceding table is from *Statistical Abstract of the United States*, 96th ed. Washington, D.C.: U.S. Department of Commerce, 1975. P. 347.)

11. *Query*: "Which is higher in protein, skim milk or eggs?"

Answer: ______________________

Nutritive Value of Foods (Calories, Proteins, etc.)

Source: Home and Garden Bulletin No. 72, U.S. Department of Agriculture

Available for 75c from Supt. of Documents, U.S. Government Printing Office, Washington, D.C.20402

Food	Measure	Water %	Food Energy (Calories)	Protein (grams)	Fat (grams)	Carbohydrate (grams)	Calcium (mg)	Iron (mg)	Vit. A (I.U.)	Thiamin (mg)	Riboflavin (mg)	Niacin (mg)	Ascorbic acid (mg)
Milk, Cream, Cheese													
Milk, fluid, whole, 3.5% fat	1 cup	87	160	9	9	12	288	0.1	350	0.07	0.41	0.2	2
Milk, fluid nonfat (skim)	1 cup	90	90	9	T	12	296	1	10	.09	.44	.2	2
Buttermilk, fluid, cultured, made from skim milk	1 cup	90	90	9	T	12	296	.1	10	.10	.44	.2	2
Cheese Roquefort type	1 oz.	40	105	6	9	1	89	.1	350	.01	.17	.3	0
Cheese, Cottage, creamed	12 oz.	78	360	46	14	10	320	1.0	580	.10	.85	.3	0
Cream, half-and-half	1 cup	80	325	8	28	11	261	.1	1,160	.07	.39	.1	2
Cream, heavy	1 cup	57	840	5	90	7	179	.1	3,670	.05	.26	.1	2
Custard, baked	1 cup	77	305	14	15	29	297	1.1	930	.11	.50	.3	1
Yoghurt, whole milk	1 cup	88	150	7	8	12	272	.1	340	.07	.39	.2	2
Eggs (large)													
Raw	1 egg	74	80	6	6	T	27	1.1	590	.05	.15	T	0
Scrambled (milk and fat)	1 egg	72	110	7	8	1	51	1.1	690	.05	.18	T	0
Meat, Poultry													
Bacon	2 sli.	8	90	5	8	1	2	.5	0	.08	.05	.8	...
Beef, lean and fat	3 oz.	53	245	23	16	0	10	2.9	30	.04	.18	3.5	. .
Hamburger, regular	3 oz.	54	245	21	17	0	9	2.7	30	.07	.18	4.6	...
Steak, broiled, lean and fat	3 oz.	44	330	20	27	0	9	2.5	50	.05	.16	4.0	...
Corned beef	3 oz.	59	185	22	10	0	17	3.7	20	.01	.20	2.9	...
Chicken, cooked:													
Flesh only, broiled	3 oz.	71	115	20	3	0	8	1.4	80	.05	.16	7.4	...
With bone, ½ breast, fried	3.3 oz.	58	155	25	5	1	9	1.3	70	.04	.17	11.2	...
Chicken, potpie, baked	8 oz.	57	535	23	31	42	68	3.0	3,020	.25	.26	4.1	5
Lamb chop, thick with bone	4.8 oz.	47	400	25	33	0	10	1.5	...	.14	.25	5.6	...
Lamb, lean and fat	3 oz.	54	235	22	16	0	9	1.4	...	.13	.23	4.7	...
Liver, beef, fried	2 oz.	57	130	15	6	3	6	5.0	30,280	.15	2.37	9.4	15
Ham, light cure, lean	3 oz.	54	245	18	19	0	8	2.2	0	.40	.16	3.1	...
Boiled ham, sliced	2 oz.	59	135	11	10	0	6	1.6	0	.25	.09	1.5	...
Pork roast, lean and fat	3 oz.	46	310	21	24	0	9	2.7	0	.78	.22	4.7	...
Frankfurter, heated	2 oz.	57	170	7	15	1	3	.8	...	.08	.11	1.4	...
Veal cutlet	3 oz.	60	185	23	9	...	9	2.7	...	.06	.21	4.6	...
Veal roast	3 oz.	55	230	23	14	0	10	2.9	...	.11	.26	6.6	...
Fish													
Bluefish, baked with fat	3 oz.	68	135	22	4	0	25	.6	40	.09	.08	1.6	...
Clams, raw, meat only	3 oz.	82	65	11	1	2	59	5.2	90	.08	.15	1.1	8
Crabmeat, canned	3 oz.	77	85	15	2	1	38	.7	...	.07	.07	1.6	...
Oyster, raw, meat	1 cup	85	160	20	4	8	226	13.2	740	.33	.43	6.0	...
Salmon, pink, canned	3 oz.	71	120	17	5	0	167	.7	60	.03	.16	6.8	...
Shrimp, canned, meat	3 oz.	70	100	21	1	1	98	2.6	50	.01	.03	1.5	...
Swordfish, broiled with butter	3 oz.	65	150	24	5	0	23	1.1	1,750	.03	.04	9.3	...
Tuna, canned in oil	3 oz.	61	170	24	7	0	7	1.6	70	.04	.10	10.1	...
Nuts													
Almonds, shelled, whole	1 cup	5	850	26	77	28	332	6.7	0	.34	1.31	5.0	T
Cashew nuts, roasted	1 cup	5	785	24	64	41	53	5.3	140	.60	.35	2.5	...
Peanuts, roasted	1 cup	2	840	37	72	27	107	3.0	...	.46	.19	24.7	0
Pecans, halves	1 cup	3	740	10	77	16	79	2.6	140	.93	.14	1.0	2
Walnuts, black or native, chopped	1 cup	3	790	26	75	19	T	7.6	380	.28	.14	.9	...
Vegetables & Produce													
Asparagus, cooked, spears	4 sp.	94	10	1	T	2	13	.4	540	.10	.11	.8	16
Asparagus, canned	1 cup	94	45	5	1	7	44	4.1	1,240	.15	.22	2.0	37
Beans, lima, immature, cooked	1 cup	71	190	13	1	34	80	4.3	480	.31	.17	2.2	29
Beans, snap, green, cooked	1 cup	92	30	2	T	7	63	.8	680	.09	.11	.6	15
Beans, snap, canned, green	1 cup	94	45	2	T	10	81	2.9	690	.07	.10	.7	10
Beans, snap, yellow or wax	1 cup	93	30	2	T	6	63	0.8	290	.09	.11	.6	16
Beans, sprouted mung, cooked	1 cup	91	35	4	T	7	21	1.1	30	.11	.13	.9	8
Beets, cooked	2 beets	91	30	1	T	7	14	.5	20	.03	.04	.3	6
Broccoli, cooked	1 stalk	91	45	6	1	8	158	1.4	4,500	.16	.36	1.4	162
Brussels sprouts, cooked	1 cup	88	55	7	1	10	50	1.7	810	.12	.22	1.2	135
Cabbage, raw, shredded	1 cup	92	15	1	T	4	34	.3	90	.04	.04	.2	33

(*continued*)

11. *Query* (*continued*)

Nutritive Value of Foods (Calories, Proteins, etc.)

Source: Home and Garden Bulletin No. 72, U.S.Department of Agriculture

Available for 75c from Supt. of Documents, U.S.Government Printing Office, Washington, D.C.20402

	Measure	Water %	Food Energy (Calories)	Protein (grams)	Fat (grams)	Carbohydrate (grams)	Calcium (mg)	Iron (mg)	Vit. A (I.U.)	Thiamin (mg)	Riboflavin (mg)	Niacin (mg)	Ascorbic acid (mg)
Vegetables and Produce													
Cabbage, cooked	1 cup	94	30	2	T	6	64	.4	190	.06	.06	.4	48
Carrot, raw 5½ by 1 in.	One	88	20	1	T	5	18	.4	5,500	.03	.03	.3	4
Carrots, cooked, diced	1 cup	91	45	1	T	10	48	.9	15,220	.08	.07	.7	9
Cauliflower, cooked, flower buds	1 cup	93	25	3	T	5	25	.8	70	.11	.10	.7	66
Celery, raw, stalk. large	1 stalk	94	5	T	T	2	16	.1	100	.01	.01	.1	4
Corn, cooked, ear 5 × 1¾ in.	1 ear	74	70	3	1	16	2	.5	310	.09	.08	1.0	7
Corn, canned	1 cup	81	170	5	2	40	10	1.0	690	.07	.12	2.3	13
Cucumbers, raw, pared	10 oz.	96	30	1	T	7	35	.6	T	.07	.09	.4	23
Lettuce, Boston type	1 head	95	30	3	T	6	77	4.4	2,130	.14	.13	.6	18
Mushrooms, canned	1 cup	93	40	5	T	6	15	1.2	T	.04	.60	4.8	4
Onion, mature, raw, in	One	89	40	2	T	10	30	.6	40	.04	.04	.2	11
Peas, green, cooked	1 cup	82	115	9	1	19	37	2.9	860	.44	.17	3.7	33
Peas, green, canned	1 cup	83	165	9	1	31	50	4.2	1,120	.23	.13	2.2	22
Potato, medium, baked	One	75	90	3	T	21	9	.7	T	.10	.04	1.7	20
Potato, medium, boiled in skin	One	80	105	3	T	23	10	.8	T	.13	.05	2.0	22
Potatoes, mashed, milk added	1 cup	83	125	4	1	25	47	.8	50	.16	.10	2.0	19
Potato chips, medium	10 chips	2	115	1	8	10	8	.4	T	.04	.01	1.0	3
Sauerkraut, canned	1 cup	93	45	2	T	9	85	1.2	120	.07	.09	.4	33
Spinach, cooked	1 cup	92	40	5	1	6	167	4.0	14,580	.13	.25	1.0	50
Squash, summer, diced, cooked	1 cup	96	30	2	T	7	52	.8	820	.10	.16	1.6	21
Squash, winter, baked, mashed	1 cup	81	130	4	1	32	57	1.6	8,610	.10	.27	1.4	27
Sweet potato, baked	1	64	155	2	1	36	44	1.0	8,910	.10	.07	.7	24
Sweet potato, candied 3½ by 2¼ in.	1	60	295	2	6	60	65	1.6	11,030	.10	.08	.8	17
Tomato, raw, medium	1	94	40	2	T	9	24	.9	1,640	.11	.07	1.3	42
Tomato catsup, tablespoon	1 tbsp.	69	15	T	T	4	3	.1	210	.01	.01	.2	2
Tomato juice, canned	1 cup	94	45	2	T	10	17	2.2	1,940	.12	.07	1.9	39
Fruits and Fruit Products													
Apple, medium, raw	One	85	70	T	T	18	8	.4	50	.04	.02	.1	3
Apple juice, bottled or canned	1 cup	88	120	T	T	30	15	1.5	...	.02	.05	.2	2
Applesauce, canned, sweetened	1 cup	76	230	1	T	61	10	1.3	100	.05	.03	.1	3
Banana, raw 6 by 1½ in.	1	76	100	1	T	26	10	.8	230	.06	.07	.8	12
Blueberries, raw	1 cup	83	85	1	1	21	21	1.4	140	.04	.08	.6	20
Cantaloupe, raw, medium	½ melon	91	60	1	T	14	27	.8	6,540	.08	.06	1.2	63
Cranberry sauce, sweetened, canned	1 cup	62	405	T	1	104	17	.6	60	.03	.03	.1	6
Grapefruit, raw, medium, white	½	89	45	1	T	12	19	.5	10	.05	.02	.2	44
Grapefruit juice, canned, unsweetened	1 cup	89	100	1	T	24	20	1.0	20	.07	.04	.4	84
Grapes, raw, American type	1 cup	82	65	1	1	15	15	.4	100	.05	.03	.2	3
Grapejuice, canned	1 cup	83	165	1	T	42	28	.8	...	.10	.05	.5	T
Lemon, raw, medium	One	90	20	1	T	6	19	.4	10	.03	.01	.1	39
Lemon juice, raw	1 cup	91	60	1	T	20	17	.5	50	.07	.02	.2	112
Lime juice, fresh	1 cup	90	65	1	T	22	22	.5	20	.05	.02	.2	79
Orange, raw, 2⅝ in. diam.	One	86	65	1	T	16	54	.5	260	.13	.05	.5	66
Orange juice, frozen, undiluted	6 oz. can	55	360	5	T	87	75	.9	1,620	.68	.11	2.8	360
Peach, raw, whole, medium	One	89	35	1	T	10	9	.5	1,320	.02	.05	1.0	7
Peaches, canned, halves or sliced	1 cup	79	200	1	T	52	10	.8	1,100	.02	.06	1.4	7
Pear, raw, 3 by 2½ in.	One	83	100	1	1	25	13	.5	30	.04	.07	.2	7
Pineapple, canned, sliced	Large sli.	80	90	T	T	24	13	.4	50	.09	.03	.2	8
Plums, raw, 2 in. diam.	1 plum	87	25	T	T	7	7	.3	140	.02	.02	.3	3
Prune juice, canned	1 cup	80	200	1	T	49	36	10.5	...	.03	.03	1.0	5
Raisins, seedless, pkged. ½ oz.	1 pkg.	18	40	T	T	11	9	.5	T	.02	.01	.1	T
Strawberries, raw, capped	1 cup	90	55	1	1	13	31	1.5	90	.04	.10	1.0	88
Watermelon, raw, wedge	1 wedge	93	115	2	1	27	30	2.1	2,510	.13	.13	.7	30
Grain Products													
Bagel, 3 in. diam. egg	One	32	165	6	2	28	9	1.2	30	.14	.10	1.2	0
Biscuit, baking powder	One	27	105	2	5	13	34	.4	T	.06	.06	.1	T
Bran flakes (40% bran)	1 cup	3	105	4	1	28	25	12.3	0	.14	.06	2.2	0
Bread, cracked wheat	1 loaf	35	1,190	40	10	236	399	5.0	T	.53	.41	5.9	T
Bread, enriched, French	1 loaf	31	1,315	41	14	251	195	10.0	T	1.27	1.00	11.3	T
Bread, enriched, Italian	1 loaf	32	1,250	41	4	256	77	10.0	0	1.32	.91	11.8	0
Bread, raisin, loaf	1 loaf	35	1,190	30	13	243	322	5.9	T	.23	.41	3.2	T
Bread, American, rye	1 loaf	36	1,100	41	5	236	340	7.3	0	.82	.32	6.4	0
Bread, white, enriched	1 loaf	36	1,225	39	15	229	381	11.3	T	1.13	.95	10.9	T
Cake, angel food	1 cake	34	1,645	36	1	377	603	1.9	0	.03	.70	.6	0
Cupcake, small, choc. icing	1 cake	22	130	2	5	21	47	.3	60	.01	.04	.1	T
Cake, Boston cream pie	1 pce.	35	210	4	6	34	46	.3	140	.02	.08	.1	T

(*continued*)

11. *Query* (*continued*)

Nutritive Value of Foods (Calories, Proteins, etc.)

Source: Home and Garden Bulletin No. 72, U.S.Department of Agriculture

Available for 75c from Supt. of Documents, U.S.Government Printing Office, Washington, D.C.20402

	Measure	Water %	Food Energy (Calories)	Protein (grams)	Fat (grams)	Carbohydrate (grams)	Calcium (mg)	Iron (mg)	Vit. A (I.U.)	Thiamin (mg)	Riboflavin (mg)	Niacin (mg)	Ascorbic acid (mg)
Grain Products													
Cake, pound	1 loaf	17	2,430	29	152	242	108	4.1	1,440	.15	.46	1.0	0
Saltines	4	4	50	1	1	8	2	.1	0	T	T	.1	0
Danish Pastry, round piece	1 pastry	22	275	5	15	30	33	.6	200	.05	.10	.5	T
Doughnut, cake type	One	24	125	1	6	16	13	.4	30	.05	.05	.4	T
Macaroni, enriched, cooked	1 cup	64	190	6	1	39	14	1.4	0	.23	.14	1.8	0
Noodles, enriched	1 cup	70	200	7	2	37	16	1.4	110	.22	.13	1.9	0
Oatmeal, or rolled oats, cooked	1 cup	87	130	5	2	23	22	1.4	0	.19	.05	.2	0
Pie, apple, 1/7 of 9-in. pie	1 sector	48	350	3	15	51	11	.4	40	.03	.03	.5	1
Pie, custard, 1/7 of 9-in. pie	1 sector	58	285	8	14	30	125	.8	300	.07	.21	.4	0
Pie, lemon meringue, 1/7 of 9-in. pie	1 sector	47	305	4	12	45	17	.6	200	.04	.10	.2	4
Pie, mince, 1/7 of 9-in. pie	1 sector	43	365	3	16	56	38	1.4	T	.09	.05	.5	1
Pie, pumpkin, 1/7 of 9-in. pie	1 sector	59	275	5	15	32	66	.7	3,210	.04	.13	.7	T
Pizza (cheese) 1/8 of 14 in. diam.	1 sector	45	185	7	6	27	107	.7	290	.04	.12	.7	4
Popcorn, plain	1 cup	4	25	1	T	5	1	.2	...	...	.01	.1	0
Roll, home recipe	1 roll	26	120	3	3	20	16	.7	30	.09	.09	.8	T
Spaghetti, enriched, cooked	1 cup	72	155	5	1	32	11	1.3	0	.20	.11	1.5	0
Fats, Oils													
Butter, regular	1/2 cup	16	810	1	92	1	23	0	3,750	...	...	...	0
Lard	1 cup	0	1,850	0	205	0	0	0	0	0	0	0	0
Vegetable fats	1 cup	0	1,770	0	200	0	0	0	...	0	0	0	0
Margarine	1/2 cup	16	815	1	92	1	23	0	3,750	...	...	...	0
Salad dressing, French, regular	1 tbsp.	39	65	T	6	3	2	.1	...	...	...	...	
Salad dressing, mayonnaise	1 tbsp.	15	100	T	11	T	3	.1	40	T	.01	T	...
Salad dressing, 1,000 island	1 tbsp.	32	80	T	8	3	2	.1	50	T	T	T	T
Sugars, Sweets													
Candy, milk chocolate, sweetened	1 oz.	1	145	2	9	16	65	.3	80	.02	.10	.1	T
Candy, plain fudge	1 oz.	8	115	1	4	21	22	.3	T	.01	.03	.1	T
Chocolate syrup, fudge type	1 oz.	25	125	2	5	20	48	.5	60	.02	.08	.2	T
Honey, strained or extracted	1 tbsp.	17	65	T	0	17	1	.1	0	T	.01	.1	T
Jellies	1 tbsp.	29	50	T	T	13	4	.3	T	T	.01	T	1
Sugar, brown	1 cup	2	820	0	0	212	187	7.5	0	.02	.07	.4	0
Sugar, granulated	1 cup	T	770	0	0	199	0	.2	0	0	0	0	0
Miscellaneous													
Barbecue sauce	1 cup	81	230	4	17	20	53	2.0	900	.03	.03	.8	13
Beer	12 oz.	92	150	1	0	14	18	T	...	.01	.11	2.2	...
Alcoholic beverage, 86-proof	1 1/2 fl. oz.	64	105	...	...	T	...	...	...	...	...	...	...
Cola-type beverage	12 fl. oz.	90	145	0	0	37	...	...	0	0	0	0	
Ginger ale	12 fl. oz.	92	115	0	0	29	...	...	0	0	0	0	0
Soup, cream of chicken	1 cup	85	180	7	10	15	172	.5	610	.05	.27	.7	2
Soup, tomato	1 cup	84	175	7	7	23	168	.8	1,200	.10	.25	1.3	15
Beans with pork	1 cup	84	170	8	6	22	63	2.3	650	.13	.08	1.0	3
Clam chowder	1 cup	92	80	2	3	12	34	1.0	880	.02	.02	1.0	...

T indicates a trace

(The preceding table is from *World Almanac and Book of Facts*, 1976 Edition; Copyright © Newspaper Enterprise Association, Inc., New York, N.Y., 1975. Pp. 145–146.)

12. *Query*: "How many gallons are in a barrel of fuel oil?"

a. 31–42
b. 31
c. 40
d. 42

Answer: ____________________

Tables of Equivalents

When the name of a unit is enclosed in brackets thus, [71 hand], this indicates (1) that the unit is not in general current use in the United States, or (2) that the unit is believed to be based on "custom and usage" rather than on formal definition. **See above about superior figures in Area Measure.**

Equivalents involving decimals are, in most instances, rounded off to the third decimal place except where they are exact, in which cases these exact equivalents are so designated.

Lengths

- Angstrom (A) ...... 0.1 nanometer (exactly); 0.000 1 micron (exactly); 0.000 000 1 millimeter (exactly); 0.000 000 004 inch
- 1 cable's length .... 120 fathoms; 720 feet; 219.456 meters (exactly)
- 1 centimeter (cm) .... 0.3937 inch
- 1 chain (ch) (Gunter's or surveyors) ..... 66 feet; 20.1168 meters (exactly)
- 1 chain (engineers) .. 100 feet; 30.48 meters (exactly)
- 1 decimeter (dm) .... 3.937 inches
- 1 dekameter (dam) .... 32.808 feet
- 1 fathom .... 6 feet; 1.8288 meters (exactly)
- 1 foot (ft) .... 0.3048 meters (exactly)
- 1 furlong (fur) ...... 10 chains (surveyors); 660 feet; 220 yards; $\frac{1}{8}$ statute mile; 201.168 meters
- [1 hand] .... 4 inches
- 1 inch (in) .... 2.54 centimeters (exactly)
- 1 kilometer (km) .... 0.621 mile; 3,280.8 feet
- 1 league (land) .... 3 statute miles; 4.828 kilometers
- 1 link (Gunter's or surveyors) .. 7.92 inches; 0.201 meter
- 1 link (engineers) .... 1 foot; 0.305 meter
- 1 meter (m) .... 39.37 inches; 1.094 yards
- 1 micron (μ) [the Greek letter mu] .... 0.001 millimeter (exactly); 0.000 039 37 inch
- 1 mil .... 0.001 inch (exactly); 0.025 4 millimeter (exactly)
- 1 mile (mi) (statute or land) ...... 5,280 feet; 1.609 kilometers
- 1 International Nautical Mile (INM) .... 1,852 kilometers (exactly); 1.150779 statute miles; 6,076.11549 feet
- 1 millimeter (mm) .... 0.039 37 inch
- 1 nanometer (nm) .... 0.001 micron (exactly); 0.000 000 039 37 inch (exactly)
- 1 point (typography) ..... 0.013 837 inch (exactly); 0.351 millimeter
- 1 rod (rd), pole, or perch .... $16\frac{1}{2}$ feet; $5\frac{1}{2}$ yards; 5.029 meters
- 1 yard (yd) .... 0.9144 meter (exactly)

Areas or Surfaces

- 1 acre .... 43,560 square feet; 4,840 square yards; 0.405 hectare
- 1 are (a) .... 119.599 square yards; 0.025 acre
- 1 hectare (ha) .... 2.171 acres
- [1 square (building)] .... 100 square feet
- 1 square centimeter (cm^2) .... 0.155 square inch
- 1 square decimeter (dm^2) ..... 15.500 square inches
- 1 square foot (ft^2) ...... 929.030 square centimeters
- 1 square inch (in^2) .... 6.452 square centimeters
- 1 square kilometer (km^2) . 247.105 acres; 0.386 square mile
- 1 square meter (m^2) ..... 1,196 square yards; 10.764 square feet
- 1 square mile (mi^2) .... 258.999 hectares
- 1 square millimeter (mm^2) .... 0.002 square inch
- 1 square rod (rd^2) sq. pole, or sq. perch .... 25.293 square meters
- 1 square yard (yd^2) .... 0.836 square meter

Capacities or Volumes

- 1 barrel (bbl) liquid .... 31 to 42 gallons°

°There are a variety of "barrels," established by law or usage. For example: federal taxes on fermented liquors are based on a barrel of 31 gallons: many state laws fix the "barrel for liquids" as $31\frac{1}{2}$ gallons; one state fixes a 36-gallon barrel for cistern measurement; federal law recognizes a 40-gallon barrel for "proof spirits"; by custom, 42 gallons comprise a barrel of crude oil or petroleum products for statistical purposes, and this equivalent is recognized "for liquids" by four states.

- 1 barrel (bbl), standard, for fruits, vegetables, and other dry commodities except dry cranberries .... 7,056 cubic inches; 105 dry quarts; 3.281 bushels, struck measure
- 1 barrel (bbl), standard, cranberry .... 5,826 cubic inches; $86\frac{45}{64}$ dry quarts; 2.709 bushels, struck measure
- 1 bushel (bu) (U.S.) (struck measure) ...... 2,150.42 cubic inches (exactly); 35.238 liters
- [1 bushel, heaped (U.S.)] 2,747.715 cubic inches; 1.278 bushels, struck measure°

°Frequently recognized as $1\frac{1}{4}$ bushels, struck measure

- [1 bushel (bu) (British Imperial) (struck measure)] .... 1.032 U.S. bushels, struck measure; 2,219.36 cubic inches
- 1 cord (cd) (firewood) .... 128 cubic feet
- 1 cubic centimeter (cm^3) .... 0.061 cubic inch
- 1 cubic decimeter (dm^3) .... 61.024 cubic inches
- 1 cubic inch (in^3) .... 0.554 fluid ounce; 4.433 fluid drams; 16.387 cubic centimeters
- 1 cubic foot (ft^3) .... 7.481 gallons; 28.317 cubic decimeters
- 1 cubic meter (m^3) .... 1.308 cubic yards
- 1 cubic yard (yd^3) .... 0.765 cubic meter
- 1 cup, measuring .... 8 fluid ounces; $\frac{1}{2}$ liquid pint
- [1 dram, fluid (fl dr) (British)] .... 0.961 U.S. fluid dram; 0.217 cubic inch; 3.552 milliliters

(continued)

12. *Query (continued)*

1 dekaliter (dal)	2.642 gallons 1.135 pecks
1 gallon (gal) (U.S.)	231 cubic inches 3.785 liters 0.833 British gallon 128 U.S. fluid ounces
[1 gallon (gal) British Imperial]	277.42 cubic inches 1.201 U.S. gallons 4.546 liters 160 British fluid ounces
1 gill	7.219 cubic inches 4 fluid ounces 0.118 liter
1 hectoliter (hl)	26.417 gallons 2.838 bushels
1 liter	1.057 liquid quarts 0.908 dry quart 61.024 cubic inches
1 milliliter (ml)	0.271 fluid dram 16.231 minims 0.061 cubic inch
1 ounce, liquid (U.S.)	1.805 cubic inches 29.573 milliliters 1.041 British fluid ounces
[1 ounce, fluid (fl oz) (British)]	0.961 U.S. fluid ounce 1.734 cubic inches 28.412 milliliters
1 peck (pk)	8.810 liters
1 pint (pt), dry	33.600 cubic inches 0.551 liter
1 pint (pt) liquid	28.875 cubic inches (exactly) 0.473 liter
1 quart (qt) dry (U.S.)	67.201 cubic inches 1.101 liters 0.969 British quart
1 quart (qt) liquid (U.S.)	57.75 cubic in (exactly) 0.946 liter 0.833 British quart
[1 quart (qt) (British)]	69.354 cubic inches 1.032 U.S. dry quarts 1.201 U.S. liquid quarts
1 tablespoon	3 teaspoons° 4 fluid drams $\frac{1}{2}$ fluid ounce
1 teaspoon	$\frac{1}{3}$ tablespoon° $1\frac{1}{3}$ fluid drams°

°The equivalent "1 teaspoon—$1\frac{1}{3}$ fluid drams" has been found by the bureau to correspond more closely with the actual capacities of "measuring" and silver teaspoons than the equivalent "1 teaspoon—1 fluid dram" which is given by many dictionaries.

Weights or Masses

1 assay ton°° (AT)	29.167 grams

°°Used in assaying. The assay ton bears the same relation to the milligram that a ton of 2,000 pounds avoirdupois bears to the ounce troy; hence the weight in milligrams of precious metal obtained from one assay ton of ore gives directly the number of troy ounces to the net ton.

1 carat (c)	200 milligrams 3 086 grains
1 dram avoirdupois (dr avdp) gamma, see microgram	$27\frac{11}{32}$ (=27.344) grains 1.772 grams
1 grain	64.799 milligrams
1 gram	15.432 grains 0.035 ounce, avoirdupois
1 hundredweight, gross or long°°° (gross cwt)	112 pounds 50.802 kilograms
1 hundredweight, net or short (cwt. or net cwt.)	100 pounds 45.359 kilograms
1 kilogram (kg)	2.205 pounds
1 microgram (γ[the Greek letter gamma])	0.000 001 gram (exactly)
1 milligram (mg)	0.015 grain
1 ounce, avoirdupois (oz avdp)	437.5 grains (exactly) 0.911 troy ounce 28.350 grams
1 ounce troy (oz t)	480 grains 1.097 avoirdupois ounces 31.103 grams
1 pennyweight (dwt)	1.555 grams
1 pound, avoirdupois (lb avdp)	7,000 grains 1.215 troy pounds 453.592 37 grams (exactly)
1 pound, troy (lb t)	5,760 grains 0.823 avoirdupois pound 373.242 grams
1 ton, gross or long°°° (gross tn)	2,240 pound° 1.12 net tons (exactly) 1.016 metric tons

°°°The gross or long ton and hundredweight are commercially in the United States to only a limited extent, usually in restricted industrial fields. These units are the same as British "ton" and "hundredweight."

1 ton, metric (t)	2,204.623 pounds 0.984 gross ton 1.102 net tons
1 ton, net or short (sh ton)	2,000 pounds 0.893 gross ton 0.907 metric ton

Density of Gases and Vapors

Source: National Bureau of Standards (Grams per liter)

Gas	Wt.	Gas		Gas	Wt.
Acetylene	1.171	Ethylene	1.260	Methyl fluoride	1.545
Air	1.293	Fluorine	1.696	Mono methylamine	1.38
Ammonia	.759	Helium	.178	Neon	.900
Argon	1.784	Hydrogen	.090	Nitric oxide	1.341
Arsene	3.48	Hydrogen bromide	3.50	Nitrogen	1.250
Butane-iso	2.60	Hydrogen chloride	1.639	Nitrosyl chloride	2.99
Butane-n	2.519	Hydrogen iodide	5.724	Nitrous oxide	1.997
Carbon dioxide	1.977	Hydrogen selenide	3.66	Oxygen	1.429
Carbon monoxide	1.250	Hydrogen sulfide	1.539	Phosphine	1.48
Carbon oxysulfide	2.72	Krypton	3.745	Propane	2.020
Chlorine	3.214	Methane	.717	Silicon tetrafluoride	4.67
Chlorine monoxide	3.89	Methyl chloride	2.25	Sulfur dioxide	2.927
Ethane	1.356	Methyl ether	2.091	Xenon	5.897

(The preceding tables are adapted from *World Almanac and Book of Facts*, 1976 Edition; Copyright © Newspaper Enterprise Association, Inc., New York, N.Y., 1975. Pp. 797–798.)

13. *Query*: "How much Federal money was spent on food stamps in 1973?"

a. $12,165,682
b. $3,883,952,103
c. $2,121,404,604

Answer: ____________________

Food Stamps—Costs and Benefits

Source: U.S. Department of Agriculture

Fiscal Year	Average No. Persons participating per month	Value per year: Total purchase	Value per year: Bonus	Avg. bonus per participant per month: Current $	Avg. bonus per participant per month: 1967 $
1962	142,817	35,202,266	13,152,695	7.67	8.47
1965	424,652	85,471,989	32,505,096	6.38	6.75
1967	1,447,105	296,106,484	105,550,172	6.08	6.08
1968	2,211,474	451,800,893	173,142,015	6.52	6.26
1969	2,878,113	603,351,143	228,818,622	6.63	6.04
1970	4,340,030	1,089,960,761	549,663,811	10.55	9.07
1971	9,367,908	2,713,273,217	1,522,749,091	13.55	11.17
1972	11,109,074	3,308,647,916	1,797,285,786	13.48	10.77
1973	12,165,682	3,883,952,103	2,131,404,604	14.60	11.67
1974	12,895,709	4,724,267,407	2,714,070,651	17.54	11.87
1975 (9 mos.)	16,329,825	5,187,844,038	3,116,836,844	21.21	13.49

The Food Stamp Program enables low income families to buy more food of greater variety to improve their diets. If a household meets eligibility requirements (a family of 4 must have a net income lower than $570 per month), it is assigned an allotment of stamps based on the number of people in the household ($154 worth of stamps per month for 4 people). The family must pay a portion of the value of the stamps, but that portion must not exceed 30% of the net income ($122 if the family of 4 has a net income between $420 and $450). The value of the stamps in excess of the amount paid is the "bonus." the value of the free food.

(The preceding table is from *World Almanac and Book of Facts, 1976*. New York and Cleveland: Newspaper Enterprise Association, 1975. P. 143.)

ANSWERS TO EXERCISE

1. (a) $20.20. Data are given up to 1974 only.
2. (b) Approximately 46% increase. (1950 = 650, 1970 = 950)
3. (b) 21%.
4. (b) Baton Rouge, La.; $4788.
5. (d) Approximately 340% increase. (1960 = 25 billion; 1974 = 110 billion)
6. (c) About 16 persons per 100,000. No data more current than 1973.
7. (a) About 150 million passengers traveled on scheduled domestic airlines.
8. (c) About 3 million less. (1950 = 5.7 million, 1974 = 2.7 million)
9. (a) Approximately a 7% decline. (1965 = 30, 1973 = 23)
10. (c) 12,561,000 more than in 1950. 1975 figures are an estimate based on 1970 census.
11. Eggs. Skim milk has 9 grams of protein per cup; one large egg has 6 grams. To compare them exactly, you would need to determine how many large eggs are in a cup, but as it is certainly more than two, the eggs would be higher in protein. (Explanation of answer: This information is not presented in the exact form required by the query because the form of measurement for the two foods differs. However, common sense indicates that the number of eggs in a cup measure would be more than two, making eggs higher in protein. This interpretation should be thoroughly explained to the user when the answer is provided.)

12. 42. (Explanation of answer: The note explains the size of gallons for various liquids, including crude oil or petroleum products. It should be pointed out to the user that 42 gallons is largely a statistical measure, and is recognized as a liquid measure in only four states.
13. $2,131,404,604. (Explanation of answer: It is necessary to read the note to determine the difference between the "Total purchase" and "Bonus" columns. This note reveals that the bonus funds are those paid by the federal government.)

8

Query Negotiation

In previous chapters, we have discussed answering queries based on selection of the message from a query, and utilizing this message to identify reference tools to search. But often the query as initially presented by the patron is incomplete, unclear, or misleading. For such queries an incomplete or incorrect message may be identified, leading to further errors in succeeding steps of the reference process. For instance, in the query, "I'd like some books about taking photographs," the wanted descriptor is *books* and the given descriptor is *photographs*. But because this query is so broadly stated the reference librarian will probably try to clarify it through negotiation. After asking the requestor a few questions, the librarian may discover the real information need: "I would like basic materials on how to use a 35-mm camera, to be used by eighth graders who have never used 35-mm cameras before." In this, the negotiated query, the wanted is *basic materials* and the given is *35-mm cameras*. If the librarian had begun a search based on the initial request, the materials retrieved may have been too general (taking photographs rather than operating 35-mm cameras), and probably at the wrong level of sophistication.

In other cases, the message itself may be complete and correct, but additional information may be needed to interpret it or place it in a proper context. For example, in the query, "Can you find me the address of Dr. Robert Smith?" the message is easily selected. The wanted is an address, and the given is a person's name, Dr. Robert Smith. However, before beginning to search for this person's address, the librarian would probably ask the patron for more information about Dr. Smith, including where he lives, what kind of doctor he is, and whether a middle name or initial is known. By gathering additional information about him, the librarian can ensure that the Dr. Smith for whom he locates an address is the same person the client has in mind.

To clarify or gain additional information about a query, librarians use an interview technique called negotiation. The term negotiation indicates two-way communication between librarian and client. In the negotiation process, the librarian asks questions to clarify his or her own understanding of the query, and also to encourage the requestor to express the query in exact terms. By means of this exchange between librarian and requestor, a final query statement is agreed upon. From this statement an accurate message can be selected, and additional information can be used to aid in the search for an answer.

Negotiation is a pivotal step in the reference process. The decision as to whether or not negotiation is needed is made following the message selection step—identification of omissions or ambiguous components of the message can provide clues that negotiation should be performed. If negotiation is not performed at this stage, an incorrect or incomplete message will continue to be the basis for the succeeding steps of the search. An answer may be located, but it most likely will not be the answer to the client's real query. The same error can result when the librarian negotiates a query ineffectively. In this chapter we discuss clues for identifying negotiable queries and the reasons why a user's initial query may contain ambiguities or incomplete information.

WHY USERS SUBMIT QUERIES THAT REQUIRE NEGOTIATION

There are many possible reasons why a user may not initially present the librarian with a final or complete query. Robert Taylor suggests that an individual with an information need goes through basically four separate distinct phases in defining and narrowing his information need.[1] In the first stage, the information need is present but has not been consciously expressed within the individual's mind. Instead, he experiences a vague feeling of uneasiness that he should know something that he does not know. Taylor calls this the visceral need. This is followed in the second stage by a conscious recognition of the information need. In the third phase, this information need is translated into a formal statement, still for oneself. Finally, the information need is expressed as a query posed to a reference librarian, if this route is taken in seeking a solution. Taylor calls this final, fourth stage the "compromised need" because the query asked may be modified according to the requestor's expectations of the library and librarian. Frequently this involves simplifying the query, since the client may assume that his real query may be too difficult to answer.

Although the final stage is one in which the requestor expresses his or her information need to someone else, he or she may not always wait until the fourth stage to come to the reference desk. If the information need is stated in the form of a query at the first or second stages of development, when the requestor has not clearly defined it, the result will most likely be a query that is stated vaguely or ambiguously.

Ellis Mount, a science reference librarian, discusses some additional reasons why the real query may not be stated to the reference librarian.[2] It may be because the client does not want to reveal the real query, or because he does not realize the depth and quality of the library collection. Other reasons suggested by Mount are because the client lacks confidence in the reference librarian's ability, or because the person is ill at ease in posing the query or in answering questions about the query. Mount points out another problem which was also stated by Taylor: It is very difficult to put into words what you do not know.

Very rarely does a client present an incomplete or ambiguous query just to frustrate the librarian. Such a query statement is based on other factors related to the patron, the query, and the patron's feelings about libraries and reference services. It is important for a reference librarian to understand the possible motivations for asking a question indirectly or incompletely, and to be sensitive to these reasons in negotiating the query. It is the librarian's responsibility, not the requestor's, to take steps to ensure that the query is fully understood before the search begins, and to conduct the reference interview with tact and sensitivity.

[1] Robert S. Taylor. "Question-Negotiation and Information Seeking in Libraries." *College and Research Libraries* 29 (1968): 182–183.

[2] Ellis Mount. "Communication Barriers and the Reference Question." *Special Libraries* **57** (1966):575–578.

IDENTIFYING NEGOTIABLE QUERIES

Any of the reasons discussed in the previous section may result in the patron phrasing the initial query evasively or incompletely. A librarian who realizes that this occurs will be alert to clues that the initial query requires clarification before an answer can be pursued. Naturally, the librarian wants to avoid negotiation when it is not necessary. Unnecessary questioning wastes the user's time and may confuse or frustrate him. As every query does not require negotiation, it is important to be able to recognize those that do.

Initial queries which may call for negotiation can be characterized according to the types of information they lack, or by ambiguities they contain. Table 8-1, "Checklist for Identification of Negotiable Queries," summarizes these characteristics in the form of questions you should ask yourself about each query statement. If the answer to one or more of these questions is negative, it is an indication that the query may require negotiation before the search begins. In Table 8-2, this checklist is expanded by listing clues which may alert you to the fact that negotiation is needed. Also, examples are provided of initial queries in which these clues are present, and followed by the same queries in their final, negotiated form, as may be seen in Table 8-3. (Each of the clues in the tables is discussed in the following text.)

The Real Query May Not Be Asked

Some of the reasons why the query as initially asked may not be the client's real query have already been discussed. The patron may pose the

TABLE 8-1
Checklist for Identification of Negotiable Queries

Pre-search
1. Is this the real query?
2. Is the subject recognized?
3. Is the query unambiguous and complete?
4. Is the amount of information wanted specified?
5. Is the level of answer specified?
6. Are there potential constraints of language, time period, place, or type of publication?
Postsearch
7. Is the query answerable in the time available?
8. Does the query contain inaccuracies?
9. Is an acceptable answer available in the literature?

query before fully developing it in his or her mind, or may feel ill at ease in asking a question which is personal or sensitive. The patron may modify the real query due to underestimating the ability of the librarian and the library collection to provide a satisfactory answer, or because the patron does not want to appear stupid by asking an elementary question.

The inexperienced librarian can be alert for general clues which indicate that the query asked may not be the user's real query. One of these is a request for a specific reference title. When a client asks you where the *Reader's Guide* is located, the real need may be for more specific information which the client hopes to be able to locate by using the *Reader's Guide*. In this case, the *Reader's Guide* may be the only title with which the client is familiar. If the librarian can determine the real query, he or she may be able to suggest additional or more useful titles to search. On the other hand, the client may genuinely want the *Reader's Guide*, needing no additional assistance from the librarian other than directions to the index tables. Negotiation can clarify this need also.

One way to handle the preceding type of query is to point out the location of the requested reference tool, and ask whether the client needs help in locating information in the tool. If the client asks for help at this point, the real query can be discerned through further negotiation. If the client obviously does not want help, then the initial query was probably the real query.

Another clue that the real query may not have been asked is a request for a specific type of tool. For instance, the client requesting "articles on strip mining," may actually want specific figures on the amount of strip mining conducted in the U.S. last year, or perhaps any information on strip mining whether or not it appears in journal articles. A similar type of query is one which is phrased very broadly, for example, a request for "books on animals." In either case, the librarian could ask open ended questions in an attempt to gain more information about the query, such as, "What would you like to find out about animals?" or "What kind of information are you trying to locate on strip mining?"

A query for which the requestor's motivation is unclear is another clue that negotiation may be helpful. The user who asks, "Why aren't there any almanacs on the shelves?" may actually be hoping to satisfy a more specific information need. The librarian attempting to determine a user's motivation must be very cautious, however, not to give the impression of prying and should *never* ask *why* the client–patron wants the information requested. He should also be sensitive to signals communicated by the user that indicate he does not want to divulge any additional information. This caution applies in any reference interview.

TABLE 8-2
Checklist for Identification of Negotiable Queries

1. Is this the real query?

Clues	Example	
a. Request for a specific title	Initial query:	"Where is the *Reader's Guide*?"
	Negotiated query:	"I want to locate an article that explains solar heating for homes."
b. Request for a specific type of tool	Initial query:	"Where are your books on cars?"
	Negotiated query:	"I want instructions for changing the oil in my 1972 Volvo."
c. Motivation is unclear	Initial query:	"Does the library have a documents department?"
	Negotiated query:	"I'd like to find the government study summarized in this newspaper clipping."

2. Is the subject recognized?

Clues	Example	
a. The context is unclear	Initial query:	"What was Franklin really trying to do with that kite thing?"
	Negotiated query:	"What results did Benjamin Franklin expect would occur when he flew his kite in a lightning storm?"
b. Subject is unfamiliar to the librarian	Initial query:	"What is a quark?"
	Negotiated query:	"Can you locate an easy to understand article about quarks, which are a kind of particle studied by physicists?"
c. Unknown terms or unfamiliar use of terms	Initial query:	"Do you have a biography on water pollution?"
	Negotiated query:	"Do you have a bibliography of books and articles on water pollution that I can use for research on a term paper?"

3. Is the query unambiguous and complete?

Clues	Example	
a. Definition of terms is unclear	Initial query:	"Can broken plates be repaired?"
	Negotiated query:	"Is there a business in town that would repair my broken false teeth?"
b. Wanted descriptor is not clear	Initial query:	"Could you give me some information on sharks?"

c. Motivation is unclear	Initial query:	"Why doesn't the library have any up-to-date books on sex?"
	Negotiated query:	"Can you recommend a book that would explain sex to my 10-year-old?"
d. Context is unclear	Initial query:	"Where is the restaurant called 'The Bakery'?"
	Negotiated query:	"Can you give me the telephone number and address of a restaurant in Chicago called 'The Bakery'?"

4. *Is the amount of information wanted specified?*

Clues	Examples	
a. Broadly phrased query	Initial query:	"I'd like some information on water pollution."
	Negotiated query:	"I'd like one or two articles that summarize federal legislation related to water pollution control, passed in the last 5 years."
b. Generic wanted descriptor is "citations" or "document locations"	Initial query:	"Could you help me locate some references that discuss Napoleon's last 3 years on St. Helena, before he died?"
	Negotiated query:	"I would like citations for all the materials on the subject that you have in the library collection, since I'm working on a research paper for a graduate class."

5. *Is the level of answer specified?*

Clues	Examples	
a. Material exists on the subject at several levels of sophistication	Initial query:	"Could you suggest a good text on economics?"
	Negotiated query:	"I've never taken a course in the subject, and would like to do some reading on my own."

6. *Are there potential constraints of language, time period, geography, or type of publication?*

Clues	Examples	
a. Geography specified	Initial query:	"I'd like some material on U.S. history."
	Negotiated query:	"I'm specifically interested in material written about the South in the 5 years following the end of the civil war."

TABLE 8-3
Negotiated Queries Asked in Public Libraries

Queries (Initial query is given first, followed by the final form of the query after negotiation.)	Checklist categories: 1. Real query?	2. Subject recognized?	3. Unambiguous complete?	4. Amount?	5. Level?
1. "Do you have a writer's book?" "Do you have a list of greeting card publishers?"		✓	✓		
2. "Do you have a history department?" "What time did the sun set on June 20th?"	✓		✓		
3. "Can you find 1404 Charles Street?" "What is the name and telephone number of the person residing at that address?"			✓		
4. "Do you have a *Books In Print*?" "Do you have a list of magazines published in the U.S.?"	✓				
5. "Do you carry a series of law briefs?" "Do you have the written opinions on the *Miranda* case?"			✓		
6. "Do you have pictures of towns?" "Do you have any information on Beaumont, Texas? Our family may move there and I need information on the cost-of-living, etc."			✓		
7. "Where can I find information on colleges?" "Where can I find college addresses?"			✓		
8. "Who was the King of France in 1840? Charles?" "Who was Charles de Morny?"	✓		✓		
9. "Do you have any information on data processing?" "I have to do a report on the effect of computers on civilization. Do you have any information on this?"			✓	✓	✓
10. "Where are your educational periodicals?" [illegible]	✓				

11. "Do you have this book: *On Death and Dying*?" "Do you have three poems on death? Do you have other material for a report on death?"					
12. "Do you have anything on lost and found?" "Do you have any information on the origin of the concept of 'lost and found'? Where did the idea of having a place to reclaim a lost article come from?"			√		
13. "Do you have a magnifying glass, I need to find something on a map?" "Can you help me find San Pedro, Honduras, on a map?"	√				
14. "Is it Broadmore Hotel or Broadmoor Hotel?" "Can you give me a name of a hotel in Colorado Springs, Colorado?"		√	√		
15. "I'm looking for books with business in them, you do know what I mean, don't you?" 'Do you have any books on shorthand?"		√	√		
16. "Do you have any books in Polish?" "Do you have the address of the Polish-American club in this area?"	√			√	
17. "Can you give me the name of the clown that ran for Congress?" "Can you give me the name of the real clown that ran for Congress?"		√	√		
18. "Do you have copies of Investigation Report No. 47 and No. 50?" "Do you have copies of Investigation Report No. 47 and No. 50 from the Florida Department of Geology?"		√	√		
19. "Do you have a book on genealogy?" "Do you have a book on gynecology?"	√				√

Is the Subject Recognized?

Frequently the requestor may have a more thorough understanding of the subject of the query than the librarian. Often you can answer queries in a discipline without knowing anything about the discipline itself, but in other situations you may need some understanding of the subject field involved before pursuing an answer. The requestor may use terms in an unfamiliar way or in an unclear context. In such cases, do not hesitate to ask the patron for clarification or for more information.

You may find that some clients cannot give you any additional information because they may not be familiar with the subject field either. This sometimes occurs when you are dealing with a surrogate client such as a secretary relaying a query for a boss. In such cases, look up the given terms in a dictionary or encyclopedia. If you have no idea of the discipline involved, begin with general dictionaries or encyclopedias, and then search special subject titles.

Ambiguity or Incompleteness in the Query Statement

The query statement may contain words that have several possible meanings. "Plates" may be a set of false teeth, bases in a baseball game, or photographic equipment. Sometimes combinations of terms are stated ambiguously. Does "chemical reactions of acids and bases" mean reactions between acids and bases, or does it mean reactions of acids and reactions of bases? When ambiguity is present it is best to try to clarify your understanding of the terms by asking the client to explain words or phrases in the query statement. The client's response to an open-ended question such as, "What kind of plates are you thinking of?" may help to avoid misinterpretation.

Negotiation is also required when the wanted descriptor is unclear or too broadly stated. For example, the query statement, "I want to find out about electron microscopes," would have to be negotiated to determine a specific wanted descriptor. Does the client want to know how electron microscopes work? What they look like? How they are used? A question such as, "What would you like to know about electron microscopes?" is likely to encourage the client to further explain his request.

Amount of Information Needed Is Not Specified

A broadly phrased query can also fail to specify the amount of information the requestor anticipates receiving. Queries in which background information is requested, or in which the wanted descriptor is unclear, as in a request for "information on sharks," must be negotiated to determine how much information the requestor really needs. The library may have dozens of books, journal articles, and other materials on sharks. A similar problem occurs with a request for citations on a specific subject, which could be answered with 10 citations or with 50. To avoid overwhelming the user with too much information—or disappointing him or her with too little—the amount of information anticipated should be negotiated. In some cases, negotiation questions aimed to determine the amount of information needed will reveal a more specific query, such as "How much does an adult male hammerhead shark weigh?"

Level of Answer Is Not Specified

For some types of queries, many possible correct answers exist, at different levels of difficulty. Requests for background information are particularly dependent on the user's background and training. If answers are available on several levels of sophistication, in a request for background information on laser beams for instance, you should try to determine whether the information will be used by a specialist in the field, a specialist in another field, an educated layman, or a layman with little formal education. Be certain to use tact when inquiring about a person's background or knowledge. It may be a sensitive point. The information can sometimes be gained by means of indirect questions such as, "Have you read much about this topic before?"

Constraints of Language, Time Period, Place, or Type of Publication May Be Needed

The subject of the query may be stated accurately and completely but the number of potentially relevant answers, documents, or citations may be too large for the client to read or for the reference librarian to collect. When this is the case, ask the client whether the query can be delimited according to language, time period, geography, or type of publication. This type of negotiation is typically used in requests for background information or bibliographies. For example, requests for references to an internationally known author might be made more manageable in this way.

Subject requests on topics for which there are numerous possible references might also be delimited by language (e.g., English only), time period (e.g., during the last 5 years), geography (only in the U.S.), or type of publication (journal articles only). This will help both in satisfying the client's real needs (too much information may be just as unacceptable as insufficient information) and may make the request for information answerable in the time available. In cases where you discover that the client does not want the search limited in this way, your own time limitations may require that you let the user complete the search himself, after pointing out potentially useful materials to him. When this is done, you should also assure the user that you will be available for additional assistance if any questions or problems develop during the course of his or her search.

POSTSEARCH NEGOTIATION

The negotiation situations discussed in Numbers 1–6 on the Checklist for Identification of Negotiable Queries involve pre-search negotiation—negotiation conducted before the search begins. Actually, negotiation appears at two places on the flowchart of the reference process: following the message selection step (pre-search negotiation), and as renegotiation following delivery of the answer to the user (postsearch negotiation).

The need for renegotiation of the query frequently becomes evident as the librarian searches reference sources for the requested information. During a preliminary search it may become apparent that the query will require time-consuming research and analysis, that the query statement itself contains inaccuracies, or that an unacceptable answer or no answer is found. When such problems become apparent, renegotiation, or postsearch negotiation, may be conducted to clarify alternatives. It should be pointed out that although the clues for postsearch negotiation, discussed in the section that follows, are commonly recognized during a search or after its completion, they may also occur in the pre-search stages of some queries.

The Query Will Require More Search Time Than You Can Spend on it

Occasionally a user will request information that is so complicated or obscure that it will require a great deal of search time to locate. Some of these queries may be of a research nature, such as the request for a comparison between the health of Napoleon I during his Russian campaign and his health as described in Tolstoy's novel, *War and Peace*. Other queries in this category include requests for obscure combinations of information, which may or may not be available in the literature. An example would be a request for the names of all currently employed female state librarians who attended library schools in the South. Each of these queries may have answers in the documented literature, but these answers may be difficult and time consuming to identify.

Negotiation can aid the librarian in satisfying such queries by first determining whether the query as initially asked is the real query. If this is the case, the librarian should conduct a preliminary search to determine whether the answer will require time-consuming research and analysis. If so, demands on your time at the reference desk may mean that you cannot afford to spend the time required to answer the query. This does not mean, however, that you cannot assist the requestor in locating the information. To aid the user in completing the search by himself, you should identify potentially useful materials, making sure the user understands how to use them before ending the interview. This is another instance in which you should reassure the user that you are available for additional help if needed.

In some cases, once the user realizes that the search may be complicated and time consuming, he or she may be willing to redefine the request to avoid having to conduct a lengthy search himself. When this occurs, the librarian and requestor may be able to renegotiate the query to a form answerable in the time the librarian has available.

Inaccuracies in the Original Query

Occasionally in searching for an answer, you will discover that the original query contained inaccurate information. In the request for an address for Dr. Robert Smith, for example, you may have determined through presearch negotiation that Dr. Smith is a veterinarian practicing somewhere in Atlanta, Georgia. In your search you may not be able to locate a veterinarian in Atlanta named Robert Smith, but instead identify one by the name of Richard Smith. Renegotiation can help you determine whether the requestor may have been uncertain of the doctor's first name, and whether the original information provided could have been incorrect. In addition to errors in personal names, patrons may also inadvertantly provide inaccurate information about pronunciation or spelling of terms, about dates, places, and other background information. The librarian who lacks familiarity with the subject may not recognize possible errors until the search reveals inconsistencies.

Search Reveals No Answer or an Unacceptable Answer

In attempting to answer some queries, the librarian may determine that no suitable answer is available in the literature. At least two types of queries fall into this category: requests for confidential information, and queries about undetermined future events. Requests for confidential information can include those for trade secrets, such as the formula for making Coca Cola, or those for classified information, such as a request for the names of individuals involved in a specific Central Intelligence Agency activity.

Although answers to these queries may be unavailable, the librarian may be able to locate related information that would satisfy the requestor. Once you recognize that you are dealing with confidential information, you can work with the requestor to renegotiate the query into an answerable form. Perhaps you can locate related nonconfidential information about the subject which would be acceptable as an alternate answer. For example, while the formula for Coca Cola is a closely guarded secret, other information related to the formula may be available which would be helpful to the user: the date when the formula was developed, a general description of the ingredients in Coca Cola (without exact proportions), or information about the number of people with access to the formula. Negotiation can clarify whether such alternate answers may be satisfactory.

Examples of queries concerning undetermined future events can include requests for figures on future petroleum production and consumption, or for the site of the American Library Association annual meeting 10 years hence! By negotiating these queries, you may be able to identify alternate requests for which acceptable answers can be found. Suitable answers may be speculative rather than factual, for example, the most current estimate of future petroleum production and consumption. In other cases, you may provide a partial answer to the original query based on currently available information. You may be able to identify designated sites for the next three ALA annual conferences, and also provide the requestor with the name and address of an individual to contact at ALA headquarters who might be able to provide further information.

In some cases, an answer to the query is documented in the recorded literature, but is not available in the form anticipated by the user. Some of these situations have been discussed in Chapter 7 on answer selection, and include cases in which several possibly correct answers are located, or in which the answer is indicated but not explicitly stated in the form requested. When delivering such an answer to the patron, the librarian should renegotiate the query to determine whether the answer is suitable in the form located, or whether additional searching is needed.

SUMMARY

In this chapter, we have discussed reasons why library users may ask queries that require negotiation, and clues for identifying negotiable queries.

A librarian should not attempt to negotiate every query asked of him or her, but should learn to determine when negotiation is probably needed. In this way, neither the requestor's or the librarian's time will be wasted by unnecessary negotiation. At the same time, any query that requires elaboration can be pursued by the librarian before a search begins.

In the next chapter, specific techniques for conducting a successful negotiation interview will be discussed. These techniques will provide guidelines for helping the patron feel at ease and for successfully clarifying a negotiable query.

QUESTIONS FOR DISCUSSION

What are some types of queries that may not have answers documented in the literature?

Are there queries that might be answerable in the literature but that are better answered in some other way?

Have there been times when you felt reluctant to divulge your information needs to a librarian? Why or why not?

How would you rate librarians you have observed in terms of determining when negotiation is needed before a query can be answered?

EXERCISE: Identifying Negotiable Queries

(The queries listed below are real queries asked of practicing reference librarians. Most were actually negotiated by the librarians, but only the query as initially received has been given below.
For each negotiable query statement, write the number of one or more reasons for negotiating using the Checklist for Identifying Negotiable Queries. If a query can be answered without negotiation, place a check in the second column.)

Sample Query Statements	*Number(s) on checklist*	*Negotiation not required*
A. *Do you have a legal section?*	1	
B. *What is the name and mailing address of the Librarian of Congress?*		X

Queries

1. "Do you have anything on translating?"
2. "Where are your college catalogs?"

Queries	*Number(s) on checklist*	*Negotiation not required*
3. "Have this year's almanacs come out yet?"		
4. "Please tell me the local unemployment."		
5. "Where is *Poor Richard's Almanac*?"		
6. "I'm looking for a source book of publishers."		
7. Can you give me the release date of the movie, 'It's a Mad, Mad, Mad, Mad World?'"		
8. "Can you give me the name of the trick where you pull a tablecloth out from under dishes on a table?"		
9. "Where do I find the cross-references?"		
10. "What is the tallest building in the United States?"		

ANSWERS TO EXERCISE

1. 3, 4, 5
2. 1
3. 1
4. 3
5. 1
6. 3
7. Negotiation not required
8. 3
9. 3
10. Negotiation not required

9

Negotiation Techniques

The first step in successful negotiation is identifying queries that require negotiation and eliminating those that do not. Alertness to clues in the initial query statement helps the librarian to distinguish these two classes of queries. If a query has been recognized as one requiring clarification the librarian begins the second stage of the negotiation process—the interview itself.

Much of a librarian's success in negotiation depends on his or her tact, sensitivity to others, and general communication skills. Many librarians who are skilled negotiators ask questions of the client based on intuition and past experience with similar requests. Although each librarian develops a personal style for negotiation, and each client request must be treated individually, some general techniques have been identified that help the client feel at ease and aid in fully clarifying the query. These points will be discussed in the pages that follow and are summarized in Table 9-1, "Checklist for Evaluating Negotiation."

TABLE 9-1
Checklist for Evaluating Negotiation

Good negotiation	Poor negotiation
• Librarian uses open questions in the initial stages of negotiation.	• Librarian interrupts patron as he attempts to discuss his information needs.
• Encourages patron to discuss his information needs.	• Uses closed questions too early in the interview.
• Summarizes or paraphrases the patron's query to insure mutual understanding.	• Doesn't give patron full attention.
• Makes eye contact with patron.	• Reacts subjectively to the content of the query.
• Gives patron full attention.	• Is too quick to state that the query cannot be answered.
• Remains objective about the content of the query.	• Provides an answer to the query prematurely without thorough consideration.
• Attempts to make patron feel at ease.	• Places patron on the defensive.
• Follows the patron's train of thought.	• Exhibits uneasiness in working with patrons.
• Shows empathy for the patron.	
• Reacts to nonverbal clues.	

OBJECTIVE OF NEGOTIATION

The objective of negotiation is to find out as much about the client's real query as possible. For this goal to be accomplished, the librarian must encourage the client to freely and comfortably discuss his or her information request. During negotiation the client, not the librarian, should do most of the talking. This is because at this point in the reference interchange it is the client, not the librarian, who has the best understanding of what information is needed and how it will be used. If the librarian is to gain a fuller understanding of this information need, he or she must listen rather than dominate the discussion. As the requestor describes the information need, the librarian asks questions to clarify ambiguities, to encourage the client to continue talking, and to determine the amount of information desired, the level of answer which will be most useful, or any special limitations on the desired answer, such as language or time period.

Geraldine King has suggested that the reference interview is composed of two chronological segments: an initial segment in which the librarian encourages the client to fully discuss the request, and a final segment in which the librarian asks questions to relate the request to the materials available in the library.[1] In the first segment of the interview, the librarian encourages the requestor to dominate and direct the discussion. In the second, the librarian directs the discussion by asking specific questions which must be answered in order to provide a satisfactory answer in a form desired by the requestor. These specific questions include those related to the level and size of the expected answer as well as to possible limitations on the scope of the answer.

OPEN AND CLOSED QUESTIONS

King has recommended that librarians employ different questioning techniques during each of the two stages of the reference interview. She suggests that in the initial stages of negotiation the librarian ask open-ended questions to encourage the client to discuss his or her information needs. Closed questions should be avoided until the final stages of negotiation when the librarian attempts to relate the request to the library's collections.

A closed question is one in which the questioner implies a choice between possible responses. A closed question may imply an answer of either "Yes" or "No," or may offer a choice between two possibilities.

[1] King, Geraldine B. "The Reference Interview: Open and Closed Questions." *RQ* **12** (1972): 157–160.

EXAMPLE

Query:	*Can you help me find some information on UFO's?*
Negotiation questions:	*Would you prefer journal articles?* (yes or no) *Would you like information on recent sightings, or information from a historical perspective?* (Choice between two possibilities)

In an open-ended question, possible responses are not implied. Instead, the direction of the response is determined by the client. Open-ended questions typically begin with such words as what, when, how, who, or where.

EXAMPLE

Query:	*I would like some information on hair dryers.*
Negotiation question:	*What would you like to know about hair dryers?*

As open-ended questions cannot be answered with a simple "yes" or "no," they force the client to elaborate, thus providing additional information.

As an example of the use of open and closed questions, consider the case in which the client posed the following query: "Does the library have any material on sharks?" The fact that the wanted descriptor is unclear is a clue to the librarian that this query requires negotiation. However, if the librarian uses closed questions too early in this negotiation process, he or she may discourage the requestor from fully explaining the request, or may even force the discussion into an irrelevant direction and, as a result, answer the wrong query.

Perhaps the librarian in this case assumes that the requestor is writing a term paper on sharks, and responds to the initial query by asking a closed question: "Are you looking for scientific or popular materials on sharks?" Given this limited choice, the requestor is forced to choose one of the alternatives presented, answering: "Scientific material, I guess." The librarian may then direct the user to the index tables, showing how to use several indexes to biological journals, assuming the user will find these indexes helpful in writing the term paper. By asking closed questions too early in the interview, this librarian prematurely restricted the client's explanation of the request. As a result, the librarian dominated most of the discussion rather than encouraging the client to speak, and obtained minimal information about the requestor's real query.

If the same initial query had been clarified using an open-ended question, the librarian might have asked: "What kind of information about sharks are you hoping to find?" This question does not lead the client in any particular direction and forces the client to further elaborate his or her needs. In this case, the client may respond: "I want to find out what kinds of sharks live in particular parts of the world." The librarian, needing more information, asks another open question, followed by two closed questions:

Librarian: *What parts of the world are you most interested in?* (open question)
Client: *I'm interested in the waters around Florida, especially the Gulf of Mexico.*
Librarian: *You'd like to know the names of the various types of sharks that live in the Gulf of Mexico and off the Florida coast?* (closed question—yes or no)
Client: *Yes, that's it.*
Librarian: *Are the names of the sharks all you want, or would you like some additional information about them?* (closed question—choice between two alternatives)
Client: *No, I just need a list of the kinds of sharks.*
Librarian: *I think I can find that information in our reference collection. Why don't we go over to the stacks and check a couple of titles?*

The librarians in the preceding examples provided two different answers to the same initial query by using different questioning techniques in their interviews with the client. By asking closed questions prematurely, the first librarian discouraged the user from further discussing the request, made an incorrect assumption about it (untested by additional questioning), and led the user to the wrong type of answer-providing tool. It is unlikely that the user would be able to quickly or easily find the list of sharks desired by using a periodical index.

The second librarian used open questions in the preliminary stages of the interview, encouraging the user to elaborate on the request. After general probing with open questions, the second librarian used closed questions to verify his understanding of the question, and to determine how much information the user hoped to receive. Both open and closed questions have a place in the reference interview, but using them in proper sequence aids in gaining a full and accurate understanding of the real query.

EXAMPLES OF NEGOTIABLE QUERIES

Each librarian develops an individual approach to questioning clients during negotiation, and no one way of phrasing can be claimed as best for all librarians. The following examples illustrate possible ways of questioning a client to clarify a query that has been identified as negotiable (by using Table 8-1, "Identification of Negotiable Queries").

IS THIS THE REAL QUERY?

Query:	*Where is the **Reader's Guide**?*
Negotiation question:	(After showing the location) *Have you used the **Reader's Guide** before?*

IS THE SUBJECT RECOGNIZED?

Query:	*I need a diagram of a node.*
Negotiation question:	*What type of node do you have in mind?*

IS THE QUERY UNAMBIGUOUS AND COMPLETE?

Query:	*I need to know about salt free diets.*
Negotiation question:	*What type of information do you need?*

IS THE AMOUNT OF INFORMATION WANTED SPECIFIED?

Query:	*I'd like to locate some articles on photosynthesis.*
Negotiation question:	*How much material are you hoping to find?*

IS THE LEVEL OF ANSWER SPECIFIED?

Query:	*Can you recommend some books on computer programing?*
Negotiation question:	*Are you already familiar with this subject?*

LISTENING AND SUMMARIZING

We have discussed the fact that a librarian should usually do more listening than talking during negotiation. This is because it is the requestor, not the librarian, who has the best understanding of what information is needed and how it will be used. The librarian's objective is to encourage the requestor to communicate this understanding fully in order to answer the query satisfactorily. To do this, the librarian must concentrate on listening objectively to what is being said.

The first step in active listening is to stop talking. As obvious as this seems, many librarians are tempted to interrupt a client to inject comments or to ask questions. As the objective of using open questions in the interview is to encourage the requestor to talk, a librarian should allow the client to talk without interference. Patrick Penland has discussed the importance of listening to the client as long as possible without interrupting, and of taking care not to rush the pace of the interview.[2]

Genuine listening involves not only concentrating on what is being said, but also being alert to the client's tone of voice, facial expressions, and gestures. These nonverbal clues can sometimes communicate a truer meaning than the actual words being spoken.

Because listening is a crucial skill for many professionals including counselors, doctors, and lawyers, quite a bit of research has been conducted on listening as a component in the communication process. Some authors have identified common listening problems which can inhibit effective listening. Some of these listening problems which pertain to librarians include preparing a response before fully understanding what is being said, faking attention, overreacting to the requestor's method of delivery, and reacting emotionally to what is being said.[3]

Mentally preparing a response before fully understanding what is being said is a common problem. Sometimes after listening to part of a requestor's query statement, the librarian is tempted to jump to a conclusion about what the requestor really wants. Assuming we know what the requestor is going to say, we begin thinking about what we will say or ask in response. We cannot listen attentively at the same time. (This is an especially tempting response when several people have asked for the same information during a short period of time. The librarian may respond to any client who begins a query in a similar way without listening to assure that the query is actually the same.) This habit can result in the librarian making comments that are irrelevant to the requestor's real information need, or asking questions which have already been answered by the requestor. This can be embarrassing to the librarian, and discomfiting to the patron.

Faking attention is another behavior that can hinder communication between librarian and requestor. Once you have learned to provide positive feedback to a requestor, such as nodding, smiling, and eye contact, you may occasionally find yourself using this feedback to make it seem you are listening intently, when you actually have something else on your mind. As a result you will have to ask the client to repeat himself, or will ask questions which already have been answered. If faking attention becomes a habit, it can seriously affect your ability to negotiate with requestors of information.

A librarian must also guard against concentrating on elements in the requestor's delivery, rather than on the message being communicated. While

[2] Penland, Patrick R. "The Interview as Communication." *Library Occurrent* **24** (1974): 424.

[3] Barker, Larry L. *Listening Behavior*. Englewood Cliffs, N.J.: Prentice-Hall, 1971. Pp. 60–69.

it is important to remain sensitive to aspects of the requestor's delivery such as tone of voice, gestures, and eye contact, the librarian should guard against letting aspects of the requestor's delivery interfere with understanding the message. Elements such as the requestor's speech patterns, accent, mannerisms, or even physical appearance can become distractors. This, in turn, can interfere with the librarian's ability to concentrate on listening to what is being said.

Becoming emotionally involved with what the requestor is saying is another potentially destructive listening habit. Undoubtedly some clients will make statements during the course of the interview which will affect a librarian positively or negatively. It is important to guard against allowing these emotionally affecting statements to trigger lack of attention to the rest of the client's message. Such an emotional reaction can interfere with acquisition of important information which may follow.

Another technique of effective listening is to restate what the client tells you in your own words. Theodore Peck suggests summarizing or paraphrasing the client's query as a way to insure mutual understanding, and to help the librarian test his or her understanding of what is being said.[4] Paraphrasing what the user has said is helpful at the conclusion of the interview, and serves as a final check on your understanding of the query before you begin a search. Paraphrasing can also be utilized during the course of the interview, at points where you feel clarification and summary are needed before new aspects of the query are pursued.

NONVERBAL COMMUNICATION

Research has shown that much of what is communicated in an exchange between individuals is through nonverbal channels. The nonverbal exchange between client and librarian begins even before either says a word. The manner in which the user approaches the reference desk, for example, might communicate feelings of embarrassment, confidence, or impatience. Any of these states of mind may be communicated without words through facial expressions, gestures, and eye contact. A librarian should strive to remain alert to nonverbal clues projected by the requestor and to react positively and constructively to them.

In addition to being alert to the nonverbal clues communicated by the client, you should ensure that the nonverbal clues that you project are positive

[4] Peck, Theodore P. "Counseling Skills Applied to Reference Services." *RQ* **14** (1975): 234.

ones. Like the client, the librarian begins to communicate nonverbally before any words have been exchanged. An irritated facial expression in response to the client's question, "Are you the reference librarian?" transmits the message that you would rather not be bothered, just as a friendly smile to an approaching client indicates that you are anxious to help him.

You should attempt to communicate friendliness, alertness, and interest to the client nonverbally as well as verbally. Establishing eye contact helps to signal the client that you are listening to him. Nodding your head to indicate you understand what is being said can encourage talk and also help the client feel at ease. Your hands can also show your attention. If you stop typing but do not take your hands off the typewriter keys, or if you continue to shuffle through the catalog cards you were working with when approached, the client will feel he or she does not have your complete attention or that he is keeping you from more "important" tasks.

SAMPLE NEGOTIATION

The script of a sample reference interview that follows illustrates some of the negotiation techniques that have been discussed in this section.

SAMPLE NEGOTIATION

Client:	Walks slowly past the reference desk, hesitates as if considering asking a question, but starts to walk on.
Librarian:	Looks up, puts down papers he was handling. (nonverbal communication) *Did you find everything you were looking for?*
Client:	*I just wanted to find the college catalogs.*
Librarian:	Gets up from behind the desk and walks a few steps toward the catalogs. *They are on this shelf next to my desk. Were you looking for any specific catalog?*
Client:	*The University of Michigan, I think.*
Librarian:	*Here is the catalog for the University of Michigan. What type of information are you trying to find?* (open-ended question)
Client:	*I need to look up the names of two professors: Fugossi and Conroy.*
Librarian:	*What information are you hoping to find about them?* (open question)
Client:	*Well, I need to know which of them specializes in properties of coal.*
Librarian:	Nods and indicates attention. (nonverbal communication)

Client: *Actually, I'm not even sure if they work at the University of Michigan or somewhere else.*

Librarian: *Perhaps we can also look for them in another source if they're not listed in this catalog. You would like to know which of these two is a specialist in the properties of coal?* (summarizing)

Client: *Yes.*

Librarian: *Is there anything else you'd like to find out about them?* (closed question—yes or no)

Client: *Well, I should probably read a couple of articles by the one who is the coal specialist.*

Librarian: *All right, we can try to find some articles too. What type of information are you hoping to find in the articles?* (Open question)

Client: *I'm trying to write a paper for my geology class, and the professor said this guy at the University of Michigan is really well known and I could use him as a reference.*

Librarian: *What is your paper about?* (open question)

Client: *It's about coal formations.*

Librarian: *Then you'd like to read the articles by this specialist to gather material for your paper?* (summarizing)

Client: *Yes.*

Librarian: *Could you use information about coal formation from other sources as well?* (closed question—yes or no)

Client: *Oh sure. My professor was just trying to help me get started on the paper.*

Librarian: *We can find some information about coal formation in some additional sources then. How will you be treating coal formations in your paper?* (open question)

Client: *It will be about coal formations in the southeastern United States. I need to tell where they are and how long they will last.*

Librarian: *Will you cover anything else in your paper?* (closed question—yes or no)

Client: *That's all. I just have to tell how much coal there is in that region and how long it will provide us with fuel. For the rest I'm supposed to write my own analysis of how we can use it wisely.*

Librarian: *So, you need to have data on the location and amount of coal reserves in the southeastern United States?* (summarizing)

Client: *Yes, that's right.*

Librarian: After taking a book from the reference shelves: *This book shows the reserves of coal for last year. Is that current enough for your paper?* (closed question—yes or no)

Client: *Yes, that will do fine.*

Librarian: *Would you still like information about the coal specialist, or any articles written by him?* (closed question—yes or no)

Client: *Not now anyway. I may be able to do the paper without it.*

Librarian: *I'll leave you with this book then. If you need anything else, I'll be glad to help you find it.*

Client: *Okay, thanks.*

SUMMARY

In this chapter we have presented some techniques for performing negotiation, including use of open and closed questions, active listening, paraphrasing, and awareness of nonverbal clues. Of course, successful negotiation has a lot to do with your own innate communication skills and sensitivity to others, and with practice at the reference desk you will probably develop an individual style which best suits your own personality. Research in communication and in interview practices has pinpointed certain techniques, however, which should be useful to you in developing your individual approach to negotiation.

QUESTIONS FOR DISCUSSION

What would you do if a patron refused to provide you with additional information for a query that needed negotiation before you could begin a search?

What are some other factors that could inhibit effective listening, in addition to those discussed in this chapter?

How does the physical environment at the reference desk affect negotiation?

Discuss examples of good and poor negotiation techniques that you have observed in libraries.

EXERCISE: Open and Closed Questions

(Examine the questions below, and designate each as either an open-ended question or a closed question.)

SAMPLE QUERY STATEMENTS	*Open question*	*Closed question*
A. *Is this the article you wanted?*		*X*
B. *What is the topic of your paper?*	*X*	

Queries

1. "Would you be interested in reading a biography to gather further information?"
2. "How much research do you plan to do on your topic?"
3. "Where did you locate this citation?"
4. "Do you remember the name of the author of the book?"
5. "Do you prefer to read a summary of the play or the play itself?"
6. "Do you know the approximate date of publication?"
7. "How many articles on the topic would you like?"
8. "When was the dissertation first published?"
9. "Is the research you're doing for a term paper?"
10. "Do you know what city this person lives in?"

ANSWERS TO EXERCISE

1. Closed (yes or no)
2. Open
3. Open
4. Closed (yes or no)
5. Closed (choice between two possibilities)
6. Closed (yes or no)
7. Open
8. Open
9. Closed (yes or no)
10. Closed (yes or no)

ADDITIONAL READING

Boucher, Virginia. "Nonverbal Communication and the Library Reference Interview." *RQ* **16** (1976): 27–32.

Heinzkill, Richard. "Introducing Nonverbal Communication." *RQ* **11** (1972): 356–358.

Hutchins, Margaret. *Introduction to Reference Work* Chicago: American Library Association, 1944. Chapter 3: "The Reference Interview," pp. 21–29.

King, Geraldine B. "Open and Closed Questions: The Reference Interview." *RQ* **12** (1972): 157–160.

Mount, Ellis. "Communication Barriers and the Reference Question." *Special Libraries* **57** (1966): 575–578.

Peck, Theodore P. "Counseling Skills Applied to Reference Services." *RQ* **14** (1975): 233–235.

Penland, Patrick P. "The Interview as Communication." *Library Occurrent* **24** (1974): 422–424.

Shosid, Norma J. "Freud, Frug, and Feedback." *Special Libraries* **57** (1966): 561–563.

Swope, Mary Jane and Katzer, Jeffrey, "Why Don't They Ask Questions?" *RQ* **12** (1972): 161–166.

Taylor, Robert S. "The Process of Asking Questions." *American Documentation* **13** (1962): 391–396.

Taylor, Robert S. "Question-Negotiation and Information Seeking in Libraries." *College and Research Libraries* **29** (1968): 178–194.

10

On-Line Searching of Bibliographic Data Bases

When you walk into the reference department of a library today, the chances are that you will see a computer terminal. It resembles an electric typewriter and is connected to a computer that may be several thousands of miles away. The connection between the terminal and the computer is by telephone line or other communication channel, enabling you to communicate with the computer connected to it. Messages are transmitted to the computer by depressing keys on the keyboard, and are received from the computer as characters on paper or on a screen. The computer terminal can be used for any task that the computer is programmed to perform. The terminal in the reference department of a library is likely to be connected to a computer that stores indexes to bibliographic data bases in its memory. These indexes, such as the index to the *New York Times*, are in machine-readable form. A computer search of this machine-readable data is called "on-line" and interactive because you are directly connected to the computer and can send instructions and get responses from it with very little delay. The computer is shared with other users, but because of its speed it can perform tasks in seconds or less, and can service requests from a number of terminals with very little queuing or waiting time. In this chapter we shall discuss how computers are searched on-line at a terminal; one of the better-known bibliographic data bases that can be so searched; the cost of such searches; and actual as well as potential uses of on-line searches in the reference departments of libraries.

When you are searching a printed index that is not a coordinate index, such as *Resources in Education*, you first consider the access points to search, for example, authors' names or subjects. After selecting the specific authors or subjects to search, the latter with the help of a subject authority list if one is available for the index, you scan the printed indexes for the required years under each selected heading. The document codes and/or complete document citations that have been indexed under these headings are located either as a single or multiple step, again depending on the index. The abstracts and/or full documents are then checked for relevance to the subject being searched. In Chapter 6, different types of indexes were discussed. It is suggested that the section dealing with coordinate indexing, including the use of logical operators and thesauri, be reviewed.

In searching an on-line index, the initial steps of selecting access points and dates to be searched are the same as for a manual search, although in some cases the subject authority list is stored in the computer memory, allowing portions of this list to be printed out or displayed at the terminal. Because the on-line searched index is a coordinate index, individual access points may be combined to form the necessary search headings. Instead of the printed index volumes being visually scanned, the selected index in machine-readable form is called for by keying in commands at the terminal, and the selected combination of indexing terms to be searched is also keyed in. The computer responds by indicating the number of documents (postings) that meet the search specifications. The searcher can then request either all or a portion of these document surrogates to be printed at the terminal.

Document surrogates may take the form of accession numbers, document titles, bibliographic citations with indexing terms, or document abstracts. The searcher has a number of options. If the number of documents posted in response to a search statement is too small or too large, he can revise the search statement before obtaining printouts or a display of document surrogates at the terminal. The searcher may also have some or all of the document surrogates printed off-line at the physical location of the computer to be mailed to him. This is less expensive than printing them on-line because less terminal time is needed, but it does take longer to get the citations as these have to be mailed from the location of the computer.

There are several advantages to on-line searching. Coordinate index searching permits the use of combinations of descriptors selected at the time of searching the index. Rapid feedback on the number of potentially relevant documents for a given search statement permits reformulation of search statements without delay when there are too many or not enough potentially relevant documents for a given search. Another advantage is that potentially relevant document surrogates are printed out and do not have to be copied by hand. Still another advantage is that you can search keywords in abstracts or titles in addition to established subject headings, at least in some indexes.

To provide an overview of the kinds of interaction the searcher can perform with a bibliographic data base, we will describe the various commands and searches that can be performed. This description is based on the *System Development Corporation* (SDC) *ORBIT* system and will be given in general terms. For actual use of these commands and/or search statements, the operating manual of the ORBIT system (or other system used) should be consulted. The commands and search statements will be described according to their time sequence: pre-search, search, and post-search.

PRE-SEARCH

Pre-search commands and search statements are typed in at the terminal before the search is begun. Such commands include those in the COMMAND column below.

COMMAND	EXPLANATION
FILES	For a listing of bibliographic data bases that can be searched.
FILE______(Name of data base)	For connecting with the specific bibliographic data base to be searched.
EXPLAIN	To obtain a description of any database program, messages, procedure, or schedule information.
NBR	To receive an alphabetical display of terms from one or all categories neighboring a specific term in the subject authority list.
NEWS	To obtain latest data-base update and system operation information.

SEARCH

Different vendors of on-line search services use somewhat different search instructions. Our example refers to the procedure used by SDC. Either single search terms or combinations of search terms can be entered by separating individual descriptors by and, or, and not, the logical connectors or operators. The system responds by listing the number of documents indexed under the searched term or combination of search terms. If the searcher wants only a few document surrogates to be printed or displayed, the command PRINT TRIAL is issued, resulting in the printing of two citations. Examination of these two citations provides a basis for determining whether or not potentially relevant documents are being retrieved using the search terms selected. The searcher can then modify the search statement or command any number of citations to be printed, up to the total number indicated by the posting. This printing can be on-line or off-line, or a combination of on-line and off-line. On-line refers to printing at the terminal during the search session; off-line printing is done at the computer location and mailed to the searcher. Errors in keying in the search statement can be corrected before the message is sent to the computer, that is, before depressing the CR (Computer Return) key.

Search terms can be modified by deleting letters, word suffixes, or word prefixes. For example, if the spelling of an author's name can either be Smith or Smyth, the following term, "SM-TH," can be searched with a special symbol, the pound sign (#), inserted in the blank space, so that either spelling variant can be located with a single search term. In a similar way, by placing a special symbol, the semicolon, at the end of the search term CATALOG, the plural form of the word can be retrieved as well as any word with a root CATALOG-, such as CATALOGS, CATALOGER, CATALOGED, CATALOGING. These provisions are particularly useful when you are searching text without vocabulary control, such as words in titles or abstracts.

POSTSEARCH

Here are some frequently used commands given after completion of the search.

COMMAND	EXPLANATION
COMMENT	To enter messages on-line for subsequent retrieval and off-line response by search service staff.

HISTORY	A display of previous search statements.
ORDER	To order full-text copies of citations retrieved in selected data bases.
PRINT	Display of results from any completed searches. (This can be done either on-line or off-line).
STOP	Termination of the searcher–system interaction.
TIME INTERVAL	The amount of elapsed computer connect time since log-in.

Before we illustrate a sample search at the terminal, the bibliographic data base to be searched will be described. The data base we have selected is the ERIC data base, which will be described in terms of the type of documents included, the unit record (the information given for any indexed document), and available access points.

DESCRIPTION OF DATA BASE

The ERIC (Educational Resources Information Center) data base, produced by the National Institute of Education, includes government reports and journal literature on all aspects of educational research. There are two sections of this data base: reports literature (RIE), available in the SDC system named ORBIT from 1966 to date, and, secondly, journal literature (CIJE), available in the ORBIT system from 1969 to date. (ERIC is also available from vendors other than SDC). The ERIC data base is updated monthly and grows at the rate of about 30,000 documents per year.

UNIT RECORD

The unit record, a term also used in cataloging to indicate the basic information given on a catalog card, consists of the following for each document indexed by ERIC:

* Accession number
ERIC Clearinghouse Accession Number
* Clearinghouse Code
Document Title
* Authors

Sample On-Line Search of ERIC Data Base

SEARCH PRINTOUT	EXPLANATION
10. PROG: SS 2 PG (11)	The number of postings for search statement (2) is 11.
11. SS 3 /C? USER: "PRINT FULL INDENTED" 1	Here again the searcher has the choice of reformulating the search statement as search statement (3) or to issue a command related to search statement (2). A command to print one document is issued with instructions for an indented format for ease of reading.
12. ACCESSION NUMBER EJ142627 CLEARINGHOUSE ACC. NO. CG510606 TITLE FOLLOW-UP OF DISABLED PATIENTS DISCHARGED FROM A REHABILITATION CENTRE AUTHORS BRODWIN, MARTIN G. SOURCE REHABILITATION COUNSELING BULLETIN; 19; 4; 607–609 PUBLICATION DATE JUN 76 ISSUE CIJE77 INDEX TERMS * PHYSICALLY HANDICAPPED INDEX TERMS * REHABILITATION CENTERS INDEX TERMS * DAILY LIVING SKILLS INDEX TERMS * VOCATIONAL REHABILITATION INDEX TERMS * REHABILITATION COUNSELING INDEX TERMS * INDIVIDUAL CHARACTERISTICS INDEX TERMS RESEARCH PROJECTS INDEX TERMS FOLLOW-UP STUDIES INDEX TERMS THERAPY	This is the printout of the retrieved document surrogate.

Sample On-Line Search of ERIC Data Base

SEARCH PRINTOUT	EXPLANATION
INDEX TERMS BEHAVIOR PATTERNS ABSTRACT THIS ARTICLE REPORTS ON A FOLLOW-UP SURVEY OF DISABLED INDIVIDUALS DISCHARGED FROM AN AFTER-CARE HOSPITAL RESIDENCE PROGRAM, WHO HAD BEGUN A PROGRAM FOR INDEPENDENT LIVING TO SUPPORT THEIR VOCATIONAL DEVELOPMENT. MEASURES OF INDEPENDENT BEHAVIOR WERE RELATED TO CLIENT INDEPENDENCE AFTER DISCHARGE FROM THE REHABILITATION SETTING. (AUTHOR)	
13. SS 3 /C? USER: "STOP"	This system-generated question requests either a new search statement or a command. The searcher signals the end of his search by the word STOP.
14. PROG: DONE? (Y?N?) USER: Y PROG: TERMINAL SESSION FINISHED 04/06/77 6:43 A.M. (PACIFIC TIME) ELAPSED TIME ON ERIC: 0.03 HRS. TOTAL ELAPSED TIME: 0.05 HRS. PLEASE HANG UP YOUR TELEPHONE NOW GOOD BYE!	This illustrates the sign-off routine, during which the user indicates that the search is completed. The system indicates the amount of elapsed time and reminds the user to hang up the telephone lest he be surprised by a staggering telephone bill.

It should be pointed out that you are charged for computer use from the time you connect to the computer to the time you are disconnected. This is an incentive to perform the preliminary work, like looking up terms in the subject authority list, before you are on-line. You will be charged for communication network time and/or long-distance telephone time as long as the telephone is off the hook.

While on-line searching can be considered a form of reference work, some of the steps depicted in the flowchart in Chapter 1, p. 2, either do not apply in an on-line search or are performed by the computer. Here are the similarities and differences in the steps of an on-line search and the reference steps previously discussed. The initial step of message selection is the same. The client asks in person, calls in, or submits a query in writing. The message of the query is selected. If the message is incomplete and/or ambiguous, negotiation takes place. The type of answer-providing tool selected is the on-line searched bibliographic data base or bases. There is no need for a lead-in tool but the searcher needs to know the content of each available data base in order to select one or more data bases to search. The message of the query then needs to be translated into search statements (descriptors, names of authors, time, language, type of publication, and other search constraints). Answer selection is specified by the client in terms of how many document surrogates to select and how much information per document to include (accession number, document citation, indexing terms, abstract, or other information given per document). This information is not copied out manually as with other forms of reference work, but is printed out by the computer. Negotiation with the requestor takes place not only at the time a search is submitted, but also during the search when the computer indicates the number of potentially relevant documents for a given search statement, and also at the completion of the search when the user examines the search output.

The cost of an on-line search service is based primarily on two factors. (*a*) a predetermined, computer connect charge for searching a particular data base, and (*b*) the amount of computer connect-time used. Data bases like ERIC and NTIS (National Technical Information Service), prepared by federal government agencies, are less expensive than services provided by professional societies, e.g., CHEMCON (Chemical Condensates, a service offered by the American Chemical Society), or services offered by commercial organizations, e.g., the NEW YORK TIMES INDEX. The costs of printing individual abstracts and/or citations off-line also vary according to the bibliographic data base used.

The amount of connect time for a search is the other major cost factor. This depends on the complexity of the search logic, the number of search statements required, the amount of time spent in renegotiating the search with the requestor while connected to the computer, and the number of abstracts and/or citations printed on-line. For short and simple searches, communication and computer connect charges may amount to $5 or less.

Highly complex and lengthy searches may accumulate over $100 in communication and computer connect charges. The average search is likely to cost about $20. To these charges must be added the rental and/or maintenance of the terminal, supplies, costs of manuals and subject authority lists, and personnel costs including overhead. While $20 per average search may seem high, the number of hours that would be required for a corresponding manual search must be taken into consideration.

COMPARISON OF MANUAL AND ON-LINE SEARCHED INDEXES

We have discussed searching a query both manually and on-line and will briefly discuss a specific search, not as a report of a scientific study (which it is not) but more in an anecdotal manner to give you a feel for the difference in searching modes. The search used as an example is for references on the use of microforms in school libraries. In both cases, the 1976 volumes of *Resources in Education* were searched. The following descriptors for both the manual and the on-line searches were selected from the *Thesaurus of ERIC Descriptors* (New York, Macmillan Information, 1975):

Microforms
Computer Output Microfilm
Microfiche
Microfilm
School libraries
Elementary school libraries
Instructional materials centers
School study centers

For the manual searches, the two volumes of *Resources in Education* had to be searched separately.[1] Because the printed index is not a coordinate index, each of the eight descriptors had to be searched separately. Individual entries for each document indexed by descriptors had to be checked to determine whether they also related to the subject described by the other descriptors. Under documents indexed by school library descriptors, entries were checked to see whether they also dealt with microforms. For the documents indexed under microform descriptors, the entries had to be checked to determine whether they also dealt with school libraries. The manual search

[1] ERIC. *Resources in Education*. (Educational Resources Information Center semi-annual index, January–June, 1976) Washington, D.C.: U.S. Department of Health, Education and Welfare and the National Institute of Education, n.d. (Also July–December, 1976.)

took about 45 minutes and yielded four potentially relevant documents (relevance being judged on the basis of document titles and abstracts).

The on-line search was done with one search statement in which all descriptors were included as a logical product and logical sum search: (School libraries *or* Instructional materials centers *or* Elementary school libraries *or* School study centers) *and* (Microforms *or* Microfilm *or* Microfiche *or* Computer output microfilm.) Searches were for documents indexed by a descriptor from the group of microform descriptors as well as a descriptor from the group of school libraries descriptors, in addition to searches for descriptors (controlled indexing terms) in the 1-year index to *Resources in Education*. The search also called for documents in which any of the descriptors were used as either title words or words in abstracts. This on-line search yielded nine documents, four of which were potentially relevant. The on-line search took less than 5 minutes of computer connect time and about 5 minutes more to instruct the searcher. The cost was $6 at the Florida State University Library, which charges for computer connect time, telecommunications cost, and some overhead.

The comparison of manual with on-line search results proved interesting because no one document was retrieved by both the manual and on-line searches. The documents retrieved in the manual search were located under the descriptor "Microfilms." The four documents were selected because they dealt with microforms of vocational education material. While these documents were on material to be collected by school libraries, they were not indexed under "School libraries" or any of the terms related to school libraries; therefore, these documents were not selected in the on-line search. The four documents selected in the on-line search but not selected in the manual search had one or more of the descriptor words in either the title or the abstract, but had not been indexed under those descriptors. The five nonrelevant documents retrieved in the on-line search were indexed under a microform descriptor plus "Instructional materials centers." These five documents were on instructional materials centers in junior colleges or colleges, but not in school libraries. The comparison illustrates the point that while on-line searching is faster than manual searching, neither type of search is likely to yield all potentially relevant documents.

On-line searching is a process that relies on several types of organizations:

- The producer of an index who sells this product in machinable form to a vendor of a search service, such as SDC.
- The vendor who supplies the bibliographic data base in searchable form along with the necessary software package for searching and with instructions for using the system.

- The searcher at the terminal—typically someone other than the final user of the information.
- The final user of the information.

On-line searching is a rapidly expanding field. About 300 bibliographic data bases and over 30 million bibliographic records were available in 1977.[2] In 1976, over 1.2 million searches were conducted.[3] In one university library, the Florida State University, which obtains on-line search service from three sources (SDC, Lockheed Corporation, and the National Library of Medicine), 105 bibliographic data bases were available in 1977. The number of such data bases grouped by broad subject area follows:

Chemistry–Pharmacy	13
Earth Sciences	6
Environment	6
Life Sciences	12
Other Sciences	15
Books and Audiovisual Materials	5
Conference Papers	1
Dissertations	1
Government Publications	7
Patents	5
Research in Progress	8
Business	11
Education and Related Areas	6
Other Social Sciences and Humanities	9

New bibliographic data bases are added frequently to those already available. To find out what new data bases are available and also what changes are occurring in existing data bases, two journals, *Online* and *On-Line Review*, are suggested. Also, receiving the news releases issued by vendors will be of assistance in keeping current with this rapidly changing field.

APPLICATIONS OF ON-LINE SEARCHING AND SUMMARY

On-line search services represent an important technological innovation in libraries. On-line searching makes possible the searching of large biblio-

[2] Williams, Martha and Brandhorst Ted. "On-line Search Service—Education and Training." *Bulletin of the American Society for Information Science* **3** (1977): 33.

[3] Data from Williams and Brandhorst (1977): 33.

graphic data bases in a flexible and rapid fashion. Like all important technological innovations, this one is likely to have an effect on its environment, the library. For example, on-line search services make current awareness services and retrospective search services possible in libraries such as academic libraries that could not afford to provide such services without on-line searching capability. Current journals, reports and other literature could not be easily searched manually for documents of interest to individual patrons, nor could retrospective searches be made. There is just not enough library manpower available to perform such searches manually. With on-line searching, such services may be performed rapidly and relatively inexpensively.

Still, on-line search services cost money and do take some staff time, both rare commodities. A possible solution is to charge the user of on-line service for the search. While this is now the policy in most academic libraries, there is no agreement that it is a satisfactory way to meet costs. The opponents of this approach suggest that it goes against the traditional philosophy of free library service, while the proponents maintain that unless charges are made to users for on-line services, such services may not be available.

There are other questions. Should the requestor of the information be trained to do his or her own on-line searches, just as he or she frequently performs searches that make use of printed indexes? If this is desirable, how can it be facilitated? What will be the effect of on-line search services on other information services in libraries? Again, it is too early to tell, but there is an indication of at least two effects. As the user becomes more aware of what the librarian can do for him, he or she will make more extensive and sophisticated use of library services. The librarian thus has the potential of becoming a more equal partner in research and teaching. Also, the use of on-line search services makes additional demands on document delivery services, specifically interlibrary loan services, since on-line search services are likely to retrieve not only more citations than would a manual search but also more citations that are not in the library. All in all, on-line search services represent an exciting development that is likely to make the librarian's job more challenging and interesting.

QUESTIONS FOR DISCUSSION

What are the advantages and disadvantages of on-line searched indexes?

When both on-line searched indexes and printed indexes are available for the same document collection, what would be the basis for deciding which index to use?

What are actual and potential applications of on-line searched indexes in libraries?

Discuss potential effects of the availability of on-line search services on reference services.

Should patrons be charged for on-line search services?

What are possible applications of on-line searched indexes to the library literature?

As a student, what use could you make of an on-line searched index to the library literature now that such an index is available?

ADDITIONAL READING

Atherton, Pauline and Christian, Roger W. *Libraries and On-line Services.* White Plains, N.Y.: Knowledge Industry Publications, 1977.

Donati, R. "Spanning the Social Sciences and Humanities through DIALOG—Part 1." *Online* **1** (1977): 48–54.

Garoogian, Rhoda. "Library Use of the New York Times Information Bank: A Preliminary Survey." *RQ* **16** (1976): 59–64.

Morrow, Deanna I. "A Generalized Flowchart for the Use of ORBIT and Other On-Line Interactive Bibliographic Search Systems." *Journal of the American Society for Information Science* **27** (1976): 57–62.

Williams, Martha. "Networks for On-Line Data Base Access." *Journal of the American Society for Information Science* **28** (1977): 247–253.

Williams, Martha, and Brandhorst, Ted. "On-Line Search Service—Education and Training." *Bulletin of the American Society for Information Science* **3** (1977): 33–34.

Yarborough, J. "A Novice's Guide to ERIC—The Data Base of Education." *Online* **1** (1977): 24–29.

11

Conclusions

We have treated reference work as a series of decision-making steps, involving the selection of the message of the query, the selection of categories of answer-providing tools to search, the identification of specific answer-providing titles with the aid of lead-in tools, and the selection of answers from answer-providing titles. Query negotiation or renegotiation has been treated as a separate chapter. We have explained why these steps are necessary, suggested how reference librarians perform these steps, and provided exercises to develop skill in performing these steps. While answering reference queries is not always carried out in precisely this way (we do not really know how reference librarians perform their task), our approach is intended as a framework for assisting the beginner to reach minimum competence as a reference librarian. Finally, we have included a chapter on on-line searching of bibliographic data bases because we are convinced that in the not-too-distant future a computer terminal will be one of the basic tools of reference librarians, just as the encyclopedia or dictionary is today.

We hope that the steps that appear most helpful to you will be internalized, perhaps by combining several steps in one operation, as in the selection of the query message and the selection of types of answer-providing tools. If you replace some of the steps for proceeding from the receipt of the query to the provision of an answer with other ways of getting at the desired results, so be it. Reference work is still largely an art and our introduction to the topic by means of the flowchart given in Chapter 1 (p. 2) is an attempt at teaching the basics. Your own information-seeking style will come into play as you gain experience in receiving and negotiating queries, and as you become familiar with the resources in your library as well as those available to your library. To put things a bit more succinctly, this book makes no claim of making you into a reference librarian. It does introduce you to a technique of answering queries; the rest requires experience and a strong motivation to answer every query in the best way you know how.

Reference work is one of the more visible tasks performed by librarians, as far as the library user is concerned. It is also one of the most challenging and, when done well, satisfying tasks that the librarian accomplishes. It is challenging partly because of the difficulty in determining what information is really wanted and how to satisfy this information need. It is also challenging when one considers the many individuals with information needs who now do not come to the library but who could be helped by librarians. Reference work is satisfying because it is an intellectual task which keeps librarians alert in view of the variety of information requests to be satisfied, and of the changes in tools available for satisfying these requests, the introduction of on-line searched bibliographic data bases in the library being a case in point. Reference work is satisfying for another reason. Typically, immediate feedback is given by the user. When the feedback is positive, it gives one the satisfying feeling of having helped someone, whether it is a child in grammar school or a professional researcher.

But things are not all rosy and bright. As we have already mentioned, people do not always come to the reference librarian when they have an information need. There are good and bad reasons for this from the reference librarian's point of view. For one thing, as we have seen, some information needs cannot be satisfied by librarians. Not everything is recorded in the literature. Some information recorded in the literature may be out of date, and/or may be easier for the patron to locate in some other way, as for example by calling up someone who knows the answer. There are good reasons for people with an information need not to come to the library, but there are also poor reasons which reflect on the services provided by librarians. The study by Childers and Crowley concluded that at least one-third of the factual queries with a single answer asked by the clients in public libraries were answered incorrectly.[1] If we can draw some general conclu-

[1] Thomas Childers and Terence Crowley. *Information Service in Public Libraries: Two Studies*. Metuchen, N.J.: Scarecrow Press, 1971.

sions based on that study (which we may or may not be able to do, in view of the study's date and the number of libraries surveyed), we can suggest that the library clients who became aware of the fact that their queries were answered incorrectly would lose confidence in the reference staff in that library, or perhaps in libraries in general.

In conclusion, we suggest ways in which libraries can play a more significant role in the information exchange process:

1. The proper attitude of the reference librarian in answering reference queries is a professional responsibility and must be considered as such. It requires a friendly and open approach to the user, so as to discover the real information needed. It requires a careful, systematic search of the literature with accurate selection of an appropriate answer. It also includes efficient utilization of time because in the typical library situation there are more things to do than time for doing them.

2. Also related to answering queries accurately, promptly, and efficiently is a knowledge of information sources and information handling techniques, as we have discussed. This, however, is only the beginning, to get you started. Knowledge of additional information resources, including resources outside the library, such as community agencies, is obtained on the job. Reference work is performed in a dynamic and continually changing environment of information resources, and learning about these changes is a continuing task of the reference librarian.

3. Expanding the market for reference work by gaining a reputation for doing a good job will bring more patrons to the reference department, but the chances are that there will still be a large proportion of the population that either have their queries answered elsewhere or do not get answers when reference librarians could be of help. If the reference librarian is to become the professional to consult when an individual has an information need, just as the physician and the lawyer are consulted for medical and legal problems, then a concerted effort needs to be made to acquaint people with what the library can do for them. This is not something that can be accomplished overnight but will take convincing of budget decision-makers and others with information needs.

As with other professions or groups aspiring to professional status, reference librarians need to find out more about how and why they are doing what they are doing—in other words, librarians need to develop a theoretical base for their work. This is not to say that our field should attempt to become a pure science. Too much of what we are doing is now and will probably remain subjective. It is unlikely that human communication, a major component of our work, will ever be completely systematized. Nor would it be desirable for this to take place. However, research is needed to answer questions such as the following:

- Which types of queries or what aspects of queries can best be handled by librarians, nonprofessional staff, clerks, or computers?
- Are there optimum ways of teaching reference skills either in library schools or on the job?
- Are there types of queries whose answers are "buried in the literature" but which could be answered with reference tools yet to be prepared?
- What is the best way of answering specific types of queries when several alternate paths are available?
- How can we determine the degree of patron satisfaction with the answers we provide for reference queries?

It is to be hoped that you now put the different pieces together and practice your newly acquired skills.

Practice Reference Queries

The queries that follow are real queries which have actually been asked in libraries. Following the queries are the answers and the lead-in tools, access points, and answer-providing tool used in locating the answer. The answer-providing titles listed represent *one* source for locating an answer—other titles may also provide satisfactory answers.

QUERIES

1. "What are the Washington addresses of the New Zealand and Australian embassies?"
2. "Where can I locate a criticism of *1984*?"
3. "With whom did the phrase 'something for nothing' originate?"
4. "Please find me some biographical information on Alexander Campbell, founder of the Disciples of Christ."
5. "Who was Secretary of State when Sumner Welles was Assistant to the Secretary?"

6. "May I have the address of the public library in Asheville, North Carolina?"
7. "What is the birth date and birthplace of Angelica Singleton Van Buren?"
8. "Can you translate this French phrase: 'a *pleins bords*'?"
9. "Who was the Secretary of the U.S. Senate in 1977?"
10. "Could you locate a short character sketch of Shakespeare's Polonius?"
11. "What are the dimensions of a shuffleboard court?"
12. "What is the address of the Major League Baseball Players' Association?"
13. "What was Ty Cobb's lifetime batting average?"
14. "What is the address of the copyright office?"
15. "What is the circulation of the journal, *Health Care Today*?"
16. "When is Sadie Hawkins Day and what is its significance?"
17. "I would like to locate some old formulas for making different kinds of makeup."
18. "Where can I find some articles on Richard Hamilton, a contemporary artist?"
19. "In which county is Encino, California, located?"
20. "What kind of training does a millwright need?"
21. "What does the expression 'pie in the sky' mean?"
22. "What was the address of Robert Levison, a history professor in a college in California, in 1974?"
23. "How many homes had television sets in 1974?"
24. "Can you give me the address of the cosmetic company, Revlon?"
25. "Would it be proper for a woman to wear a cocktail dress to a 1:00 wedding?"
26. "Who was the Ambassador to Norway appointed by President Ford?"
27. "What determines the date of Easter?"
28. "I would like some background information about Al-Azhar University Cairo."
29. "What is the address of the Richmond, Virginia, *Times*?"
30. "I would like the names of U.S. book publishers who publish books in braille."
31. "How many books were written by Zane Grey?"
32. "Where can I find a list of serial publications of the American Medical Association?"
33. "Could you give me the address of the *Daily American*, published in Rome, Italy?"
34. "Could you give me the names and addresses of art schools in Ohio that were functioning in 1976?"

35. "Could you give me information on the accreditation and curriculum of St. Leo College in Florida?"
36. "What is the address of the main office of Publix supermarkets?"
37. "What is arteriosclerosis?"
38. "When were Kennedy half-dollars first minted?"
39. "I need the address of a company in Arkansas that manufactures folding doors."
40. "What sort of salaries do foresters make?"

ANSWERS

1. Lead-In Tool: Sheehy, *Guide to Reference Books*, p. 536

   Access Point: Political Science—Government—U.S.—Official Registers

   Answer-Providing Tool: *Official Congressional Directory*, 1977. (Washington, D.C.: U.S. Government Printing Office, 1977. P. 823 (Australia); p. 833 (New Zealand).

   Access Point: Consular Officers and Diplomatic Representatives, Foreign, in the U.S.

   Answer:
   New Zealand
   Office of the Embassy
   19 Observatory Circle
   Washington, D.C., 20008
   Australia
   Office of the Embassy
   1601 Massachusetts Avenue
   Washington, D.C., 20036

2. Lead-In Tool: Sheehy, *Guide to Reference Books*, p. 309

   Access Point: Literature—General Works—Essays—Indexes

   Answer-Providing Tool: *Essay and General Literature Index* New York: H. W. Wilson Co. Vol. 5–8, 1955–1974; vol. 5, p. 892; vol. 6, p. 984; vol. 7, p. 992; vol. 8, p. 1114

   Access Point: Orwell, George
   about individual works
   Nineteen Eighty-Four

   Answer:
   1955–1959 3 criticisms
   1960–1964 2 criticisms
   1965–1969 1 criticism
   1970–1974 2 criticisms

3. Lead-In Tool: Sheehy, *Guide to Reference Books*, p. 303

   Access Point: Literature – General Works – Quotations

Answer-Providing Tool: *Home Book of Quotations*, 8th ed. New York: Dodd Mead, 1956. P. 750:5.

Access Point: "Something: for nothing"

Answer: "To do nothing and get something formed a boy's ideal of a manly career." Benjamin Disraeli, *Sybil*, Book. i. Chap. 5. Hence, "something for nothing."

4. Lead-In Tool: Sheehy, *Guide to Reference Books*, p. 213

Access Point: Biography – United States

Answer-Providing Tool: *National Encyclopedia of American Biography*. New York: James T. White Co., 1898–). Vol. 4; p. 161.

Access Point: Campbell, Alexander, theologian

5. Lead-In Tool: Sheehy, *Guide to Reference Books*, p. 212

Access Point: Biography – International

Answer-Providing Tool: *Webster's Biographical Dictionary*. Springfield, Mass.: G. and C. Merriam Co., 1972. P. 1667.

Access Point: Welles, Sumner for dates 1933–1943. Then to chart of Cabinet members by date

Answer: Cordell Hull

6. Lead-In Tool: Sheehy, *Guide to Reference Books*, p. 85

Access Point: Librarianship and Library Resources—Directories, U.S.

Answer-Providing Tool: *American Library Directory*, 30th ed. New York: R. R. Bowker, 1976–1977. P. 768.

Access Point: North Carolina—Asheville

Answer: Pack Memorial Public Library
8 S. Pack Square
Asheville, N.C., 29901

7. Lead-In Tool: Sheehy, *Guide to Reference Books*, p. 213

Access Point: United States—Biography

Answer-Providing Tool: *National Encyclopedia of American Biography*, vol. 6, p. 434

Access Point: Van Buren, Angelica

Answer: Born Sumter District, S.C., about 1820

8. Lead-In Tool: Sheehy, *Guide to Reference Books*, p. 131

Access Point: Language Dictionaries—Foreign languages—French

Answer-Providing Tool: *New Cassell's French Dictionary*. New York: Funk and Wagnalls, 1962. P. 99.

Access Point:	*bord*
Answer:	'full to the brim'
9. Lead-In Tool:	Sheehy, *Guide to Reference Books*, p. 537
Access Point:	Political Science—Government—U.S.—Official Registers
Answer-Providing Tool:	*Official Congressional Directory*, 1977. Washington, D.C.: U.S. Government Printing Office, 1977. P. 416.
Access Point:	Senate, Officers of
Answer:	J. S. Kimmitt
10. Lead-In Tool:	Card catalog
Access Point:	Shakespare, William—Dictionaries, Indexes, etc.
Answer-Providing Tool:	*Reader's Encyclopedia of Shakespeare*. New York: Crowell, 1966. P. 650.
Access Point:	Polonius
Answer:	On page 650
11. Lead-In Tool:	Sheehy, *Guide to Reference Books*, p. 453
Access Point:	Education, Recreation and sports—Dictionaries and encyclopedia.
Answer-Providing Tool:	Menke, Frank G. *The Encyclopedia of Sports*. South Brunswick, N.J.: A. S. Barnes, 1975. P. 867.
Access Point:	Shuffleboard
Answer:	52-feet long, 6-feet wide
12. Lead-In Tool:	Sheehy, *Guide to Reference Books*, p. 435
Access Point:	General Works—Associations, Societies and Academies—U.S.
Answer-Providing Tool:	*Encyclopedia of Associations*. Detroit: Gale Research, 1978. Vol. 1; p. 1104; entry 12688.
Access Point:	Major League Baseball Players' Association
Answer:	375 Park Avenue, New York, N.Y. 10022
13. Lead-In Tool:	Card catalog
Access Point:	Athletes—American—Biographical Dictionaries
Answer-Providing Tool:	*Who Was Who in American Sports. New York:* Hawthorn, 1971. P. 52.
Access Point:	Cobb, Ty
Answer:	.367

14. Lead-In Tool: Sheehy, *Guide to Reference Books*, p. 537

Access Point: Political Science—Government—U.S.—Official Registers

Answer-Providing Tool: *U.S.Government Manual*, 1977–1978. Washington, D.C.: U.S. Government Printing Office, 1977–1978. P.60.

Access Point: Copyright Office

Answer: Register of Copyrights
10 First Street SE
Washington, D.C. 20540

15. Lead-In Tool: Sheehy, *Guide to Reference Books*, p. 161

Access Point: Periodicals—Bibliography

Answer-Providing Tool: *Ulrich's International Periodicals Directory*, 1977–1978. New York: R. R. Bowker, 1932–). P. 1655.

Access Point: *Health Care Today*

Answer: Under cessation. This journal is no longer published.

16. Lead-In Tool: Sheehy, *Guide to Reference Books*, p. 477

Access Point: Folklore and popular customs—Holidays

Answer-Providing Tool: *The American Book of Days*. New York: H. W. Wilson, 1948. P. 588.

Access Point: Sadie Hawkins Day

Answer: November 9th—Maidens and spinsters can pursue unattached males

17. Lead-In Tool: Sheehy, *Guide to Reference Books*, p. 714

Access Point: Pure and Applied Sciences—General Works—Formulas and Recipes

Answer-Providing Tool: *Henley's Twentieth Century Book of Formulas, Processes, and* Trade Secrets. New York: Henley Publishing Co., 1956. P. 225.

Access Point: Cosmetics

Answer: Formulas begin on p. 225

18. Lead-In Tool: Sheehy, *Guide to Reference Books*, p. 209

Answer-Providing Tool: *Biography Index.*NewYork, H.W. Wilson, 1974–). Vol. 7 (1964–1967), p. 258; Vol. 8. (1967–5970), p. 280; vol. 10 (1973–1976), p. 313.

Access Point: Hamilton, Richard, painter

Answer: one article 1964–1967
one article 1967–1970
one article 1973–1976

19. Lead-In Tool: Sheehy, *Guide to Reference Books*, p. 592

Access Point: Geography—Atlases—General

Answer-Providing Tool: *Rand McNally 1976 Commercial Atlas Marketing Guide.* Chicago, Rand McNally, 1976. P. 126.

Access Point: Encino, Calif.

Answer: Part of the city of Los Angeles—Los Angeles County

20. Lead-In Tool: Sheehy, *Guide to Reference Books*, p. 530

Access Point: Economics—Occupations

Answer-Providing Tool: *Occupational Outlook Handbook 1976–1977.* Washington, D.C.: U.S. Bureau of Labor Statistics, 1976. P. 64.

Access Point: Millwrights

Answer: On-the-job training or formal apprenticeship programs lasting 4 years

21. Lead-In Tool: Sheehy, *Guide to Reference Books*, pp. 117–118

Access Point: Language Dictionaries—English Language—Slang

Answer-Providing Tool: Partridge, Eric. *A Dictionary of Slang and Unconventional English.* New York: Macmillan, 1970. Pp. 372–373.

Access Point: "pie in the sky"

Answer: "Paradise; or heaven," ca. 1918, from U.S. song," "There'll be pie in the sky when you die"

22. Lead-In Tool: Sheehy, *Guide to Reference Books*, p. 450

Access Point: Education—Biography

Answer-Providing Tool: *Directory of American Scholars*, 6th ed. Lancaster, Pa: Science Press, 1974

Access Point: Levinson (note corrected spelling), Robert

Answer:
Robert E. Levinson
Department of History
San José State University
125 S. 7th Street
San José, Calif. 95192

23. Lead-In Tool: Sheehy, *Guide to Reference Books*, p. 484

Access Point: Statistics—United States—Compendiums

Answer-Providing Tool: *Statistical abstract of the United States 1975.* Washington. D.C.: U.S. Government Printing Office, 1975. P. 723.

Access Point: Television sets; Houses with

Answer:
B&W: 70.8 million
Color: 50.7 million

24. Lead-In Tool: Sheehy, *Guide to Reference Books*, p. 509

Access Point: Economics—Business—Biography

Answer-Providing Tool: *Poor's Register of Corporations, Directors, and Executives*, 1978. New York: Standard and Poor Corporation, 1978. Vol. 1; p. 1887.

Access Point: Revlon, Inc.

Answer: Revlon, Inc.
767 Fifth Ave.
New York, N.Y. 10022

25. Lead-In Tool: Sheehy, *Guide to Reference Books*, p. 478

Access Point: Etiquette—Handbooks

Answer-Providing Tool: Elizabeth L. Post, (ed.). *The New Emily Post's Etiquette*. New York: Funk and Wagnalls, 1975. Pp. 582–583.

Answer: Weddings: Clothes for Guests
Simple daytime wedding—an afternoon dress. If not attending the reception—clothes suitable for church

26. Lead-In Tool: Sheehy, *Guide to Reference Books*, p. 188

Access Point: Newspapers—Indexes—United States

Answer-Providing Tool: *New York Times Index* 1976. New York: New York Times 1976. P. 558. Refers to *New York Times* March 25, 1976, p. 41, col. 2.

Access Point: Ford, Gerald Rudolph, Jr.
Appointments

Answer: William A. Anders

27. Lead-In Tool: Sheehy, *Guide to Reference Books*, p. 485

Access Point: Statistics—Compendiums

Answer-Providing Tool: *World Almanac and Book of Facts 1976*. New York and Cleveland: Newspaper Enterprise Association, 1976. P. 495

Access Point: Easter

Answer: First Sunday following the fourteenth day of the Paschal Moon, which is the first moon whose fourteenth day comes on or after March 21.

28. Lead-In Tool: Sheehy, *Guide to Reference Books*, p. 447

Access Point: Education—General Works—Directories—International

Answer-Providing Tool: *World of Learning*, 28th ed. London: G. Allen and Unwin, 1977/78. P. 387 ff.

Answer: Begins on page 387

29. Lead-In Tool: Sheehy, *Guide to Reference Books*, pp. 162–163.

Access Point: Periodicals—Bibliography—U.S.

Answer-Providing Tool: *Ayer Directory of Publications 1978*. Philadelphia: Ayer Press, 1978. P. 859.

Access Point: Times, Virginia, Richmond

Answer: Richmond Times-Dispatch
333 East Gracie Street
Richmond Newspapers, Inc.
Richmond, VA 23219

30. Lead-In Tool: Sheehy, *Guide to Reference Books*, p. 299

Access Point: Literature—General Works—Directories

Answer-Providing Tool: *Literary Marketplace 1978*. New York: R. R. Bowker, 1978. P. 144.

Access Point: Book publishers—Braille

Answer: Several publishers are listed

31. Lead-In Tool: Sheehy, *Guide to Reference Books*, p. 301

Access Point: Literature—General Works—Biographies of Authors

Answer-Providing Tool: Stanley J. Kunitz and Howard Haycraft, (ed.). *Twentieth Century Authors*. New York: H. W. Wilson, 1942. P. 578.

Access Point: Grey, Zane

Answer: 54

32. Lead-In Tool: Sheehy, *Guideto Reference Books*, p. 435

Access Point: Social Sciences—General Works—Associations, Societies and Academies—U.S.

Answer-Providing Tool: *Encyclopedia of Associations*, 1978. Detroit, Gale Research, 1978. Vol. 1; p. 752.

Access Point: American Medical Association

Answer: Given in Section 8—Health and Medical Organizations—American Medical Association (AMA)

33. Lead-In Tool: Sheehy, *Guide to Reference Books*, p. 535

Access Point: Political Science—Yearbooks

Answer-Providing Tool: *Europa Yearbook*, 1978. London, Europa Publications, 1978. p. 888

Access Point: Italy—Press—Rome

Answer: *Daily American*
Via Due Macelli 23
Rome, Italy

34. Lead-In Tool:	Sheehy, *Guide to Reference Books*, p. 380
Access Point:	Fine Arts—General Works—Directories
Answer-Providing Tool:	*American Art Directory*, 1974–1976. New York: Macmillan, 1976. Pp. 388–393.
Access Point:	Art Schools, under Ohio
Answer:	Numerous listings
35. Lead-In Tool:	Sheehy, *Guide to Reference Books*, pp. 447–448
Access Point:	Education—General Works—Directories—U.S.
Answer-Providing Tool:	*College Blue Book*, 15th ed. New York: Macmillan, 1972. Vol. 3; p. 123.
Access Point:	Florida—St. Leo College
Answer:	On P. 123
36. Lead-In Tool:	Sheehy, *Guide to Reference Books*, p. 509
Access Point:	Economics—Business—Biography
Answer-Providing Tool:	*Poor's Register of Corporations, Directors, and Executives*, 1978. New York: Standard and Poor Corporation, 1978. Vol. 1; p. 1834.
Access Point:	Publix Super Markets Inc.
Answer:	Public Super Markets Inc. 2040 New Tampa Highway Lakeland, Florida 33802
37. Lead-In Tool:	Sheehy, *Guide to Reference Books*, p. 808
Access Point:	Medical Sciences—Medicine—Dictionaries
Answer-Providing Tool:	*Dorland's Illustrated Medical Dictionary*, 24th ed. Philadelphia. Saunders, 1900–. P. 88.
Access Point:	Arteriosclerois
Answer:	Loss of elasticity, thickening, and hardening of the arteries
38. Lead-In Tool:	Card catalog
Access Point:	Numismatics—Dictionaries
Answer-Providing Tool:	Burton Hobson and Obojski, Robert. *Illustrated Encyclopedia of World Coins*. Garden City, N.Y.: Doubleday, 1970. Pp. 468–469.
Access Point:	Kennedy half-dollar, U.S.
Answer:	February 11, 1964

39. Lead-In Tool: Sheehy, *Guide to Reference Books*, p. 527

Access Point: Economics—Manufacturers—Directories

Answer-Providing Tool: *Thomas' Register of Manufacturers*, 67th ed. 1977. Vol. 2; p. 2795.

Access Point: Doors, Folding

Answer: Dyke Industries
309 Center Street
Little Rock
Arkansas

40. Lead-In Tool: Sheehy, *Guide to Reference Books*, p. 530

Access Point: Economics—Occupations

Answer-Providing Tool: *Occupational Outlook Handbook 1976–1977*. Washington, D.C.: Washington, D.C. U.S. Government printing office, Bureau of Labor Statistics, 1976. P. 320.

Access Point: Foresters

Answer: B.A. Degree—$8500
M.S. or Experience—$10,500 Federal salaries
Ph.D.—$12,841–$15,841

Index[1]

[1] Three types of access points are included in this index: (*a*) Subjects, for example, "Query negotiation"; (*b*) Authors' names whose writings on reference work have been discussed in the text, for example, "Taylor, Robert S." (*c*) Titles of reference tools described and/or discussed in the text, for example, the "*Thesaurus of ERIC Descriptors*."

Index headings are arranged in one alphabet. The filing of headings is letter by letter rather than word by word. For example, "Indexes" is filed before "Index vocabulary aids." Acronyms are interfiled alphabetically rather than at the beginning of the letter; for example, the *ALA Yearbook* is filed after "Abstracts" rather than at the beginning of the A's.